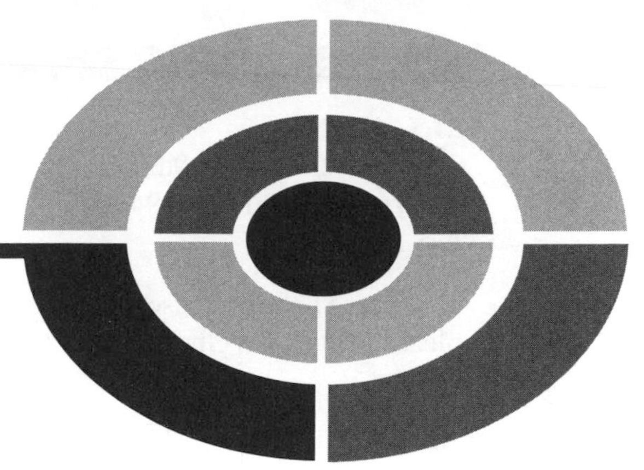

XML DEMYSTIFIED

JIM KEOGH & KEN DAVIDSON

McGraw-Hill

New York Chicago San Francisco Lisbon London
Madrid Mexico City Milan New Delhi San Juan
Seoul Singapore Sydney Toronto

The McGraw-Hill Companies

McGraw-Hill
2100 Powell Street, 10th Floor
Emeryville, California 94608
U.S.A.

To arrange bulk purchase discounts for sales promotions, premiums, or fund-raisers, please contact **McGraw-Hill** at the above address.

XML Demystified

1234567890 FGR FGR 0198765

ISBN 0-07-226210-9

Acquisitions Editor
Wendy Rinaldi

Project Manager
Patty Mon

Project Editor
Claire Splan

Acquisitions Coordinator
Alexander McDonald

Technical Editor
Todd Meister

Copy Editor
Lauren Kennedy

Proofreader
Paul Tyler

Composition and Illustration
Apollo Publishing Services

Cover Series Design
Margaret Webster-Shapiro
Handel Low

Cover Illustration
Lance Lekander

Series Design
Peter F. Hancik

This book was composed with Adobe® InDesign®.

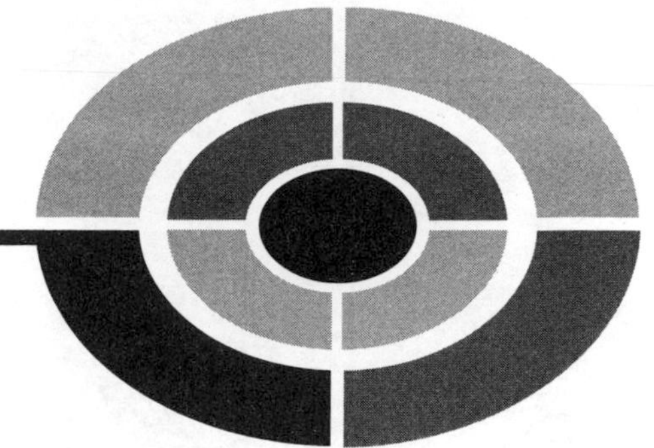

XML DEMYSTIFIED

This book is dedicated to Anne, Sandy, Joanne, Amber-Leigh Christine, and Graff, without whose help and support this book couldn't have been written.

—Jim

To Liz, Alex, Jack and Janice.

—Ken

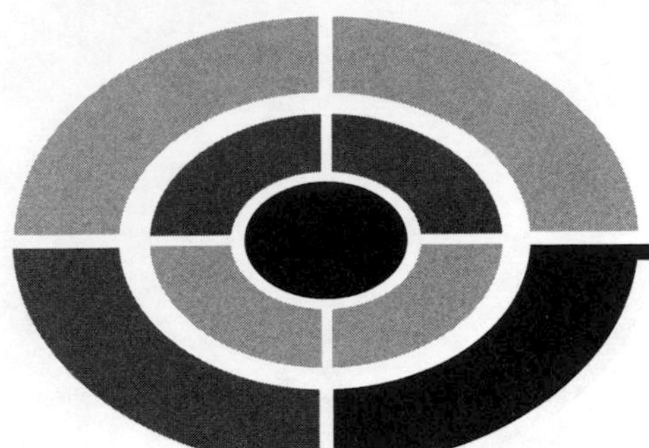

ABOUT THE AUTHORS

Jim Keogh is on the faculty of Columbia University and Saint Peter's College in Jersey City, New Jersey. He developed the e-commerce track at Columbia University. Keogh has spent decades developing applications for major Wall Street corporations and is the author of more than 60 books, including *J2EE: The Complete Reference, Java Demystified, ASP.NET Demystified, Data Structures Demystified,* and others in the *Demystified* series.

Ken Davidson is a Columbia University faculty member in the computer science department. In addition to teaching, Davidson develops applications for major corporations in both Java and C++.

CONTENTS AT A GLANCE

CONTENTS

INTRODUCTION

If you marveled at how you can use HTML to tell a browser how to display information on your web page, then you're going to be blown off your seat when you master XML. XML is a standard for creating your own markup language—you might say your own HTML. You define your own tags used to describe a document.

Why would want to create your own markup language?

Suppose you were in the insurance industry and wanted to exchange documents electronically with business partners. A markup language can be used to describe each part of the document so everyone can easily identify elements of the document electronically.

Suppose you were in the publishing industry and wanted online retailers to display information about all your books in their electronic catalog. The table of contents, author name, chapters, and other components of a book can be electronically picked apart and sent to online retailers using customized XML tags.

HTML is a standard set of tags that is universally used throughout the world. A similar set of tags can be established by an industry to describe industry-specific documents using XML. For example, the pharmaceutical industry can create a standard tag set to describe drugs such as dose, scientific name, and brand name.

Once an XML tag set is defined, you can use those tags just like you use HTML tags to create a web document. And like HTML, XML tags can be interpreted into HTML tags so your document can be displayed in a browser.

Furthermore, you can electronically:

- Parse XML documents
- Search XML document
- Create new XML documents

- Insert data into an XML document
- Remove data from an XML document
- And much more.

XML confuses many who are familiar with managing data using a database. Both a database and XML are used to manage data. However, XML is used to manage data that doesn't lend itself to a traditional database such as a legal document, a book, or an insurance policy. It just isn't easy to cram those into a formal database.

However, XML is perfect for managing that type of information because you can create your own tags that describe parts of those documents. Best of all, there are tools available that enable you to search and manipulate parts of an XML document similar to how you use a database.

XML Demystified shows you how to define your own set of markup tags using XML and how to use electronic tools to make an XML document a working part of your business.

By the end of this book you'll be able to make your own classy markup tags that will leave even the sophisticated business manager in awe—and the IT department left scratching their heads, asking: How did he do that?

A Look Inside

XML can be challenging to learn unless you follow the step-by-step approach that is used in *XML Demystified.* Topics are presented in an order in which many developers like to learn them—starting with basic components and then gradually moving on to those features found on classy websites.

Each chapter follows a time-tested formula that first explains the topic in an easy-to-read style and then shows how it is used in a working web page that you can copy and load yourself. You can then compare your web page with the image of the web page in the chapter to be assured that you've coded the web page correctly. There is little room for you to go adrift.

Chapter 1: XML: An Inside Look

No doubt you heard a lot about XML since many in the business community see XML as a revolutionary way to store, retrieve, and exchange information within a firm and among business partners. The first chapter provides you with an overview of XML before learning the nuts and bolts of applying XML to solve a real business problem.

Chapter 2: Creating an XML Document

Now that you have an understanding of what XML is and how it works, it is time to learn how to apply your knowledge and design your own set of XML markup tags. Chapter 2 shows you step by step how to create a set of XML markup tags by finding natural relationships among pieces of information in your document.

Chapter 3: Document Type Definitions

Markup tags used in an XML document conform to a standard set of markup tags that are adopted by a company or an industry. An XML standard is defined in a document type definition that specifies markup tags that can be used in the XML document and specifies the parent-child structure of those tags. Chapter 3 takes an in-depth look at how to develop your own document type definition.

Chapter 4: XML Schema

A parser is software used to extract data from an XML document. However, before doing so, the parser must learn about the XML tags used to describe data in the document by using an XML schema. In this chapter you'll learn how to create an XML schema for your XML document.

Chapter 5: XLink, XPath, XPointer

Real-world XML documents can become complex and difficult to navigate, especially if the document references multiple external resources such as other documents and images. Professional XML developers use XML's version of global position satellites to find elements within the XML document by using XLink, XPath, and XPointer. Sound confusing? Well, it won't be by the time you finish this chapter.

Chapter 6: XSLT

A common problem facing anyone who works with data is that data is usually stored in different formats. For example, some systems store a date as 1/1/09 while others store it as 01 Jan 09. However, much of this problem can be resolved by using XML because data in an XML document can be easily converted into any format by using a stylesheet. A stylesheet is a road map that shows how to convert the XML document into another format. In this chapter, you'll learn how to create a stylesheet and how to use an XSLT processor to transform an XML document into an entirely different format.

Chapter 7: XML Parsers and Transformations

The powerhouse that makes an XML document come alive is the parser. A parser can transform a bunch of characters in an XML document into anything you can imagine. There are many parsers that you can choose from. This chapter provides you with insight into each standard, enabling you to make an intelligence choice when selecting a parser to transform your XML documents.

Chapter 8: Really Simple Syndication (RSS)

If you ever wished there was a way to distribute your web content to the millions of web sites on the Internet, then you'll enjoy reading this chapter. RSS is an application of XML that is used to register your content with companies called aggregators. Aggregators are like a chain of supermarkets for web site content. In this chapter, you'll how to create an RSS document that contains all the information an aggregator requires to offer your content to other web site operators.

Chapter 9: XQuery

Think of XQuery as your electronic assistant who knows where to find any information in an XML document as fast as your computer will allow. Your job is to use the proper expression to request the information. In this chapter, you'll harness the power of XQuery by learning how to write expressions that enables you to tap into the vast treasure trove of information stored in an XML document.

Chapter 10: MSXML

MSXML is an application program interface (API) that enables you to unleash an XML document from within a program written with such programming languages as JavaScript, Visual Basic, and C++ by using Microsoft's XML Core Services, simply referred to as MSXML. Any XML document can easily be integrated into your application by calling features of MSXML from within your program. You'll learn about MSXML in this chapter and how to access an XML document using JavaScript. The same basic principle used for JavaScript can be applied to other programming languages.

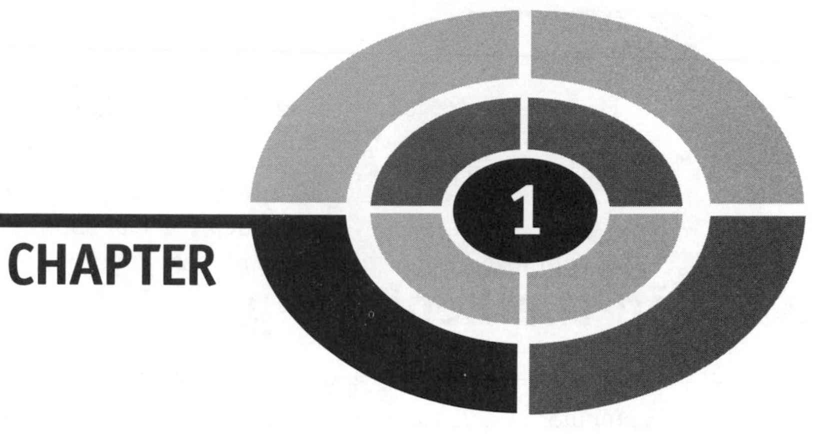

XML: An Inside Look

No doubt you've heard a lot about Extensible Markup Language (XML) since many in the business community see it as a revolutionary way to store, retrieve, and exchange information within a firm and among business partners.

Also you've probably assumed that XML has something to do with HyperText Markup Language (HTML) since the two languages have similar names—and you are correct. Both HTML and XML are markup languages that describe something. It's that something where HTML and XML go their separate ways.

HTML describes how data should look on the screen. XML describes the data itself. It sounds a bit confusing at first, but consider the title of a book. HTML might say the title should be displayed in bold italics. XML might say that this is a book title.

XML is a flexible markup language that you create yourself. That is, you decide the XML tags that describe data rather than having to adhere to a standard set of tags as you do with HTML. This flexibility enables firms and industries to create their own standard tags to describe data that's particular to their business.

However, we're getting ahead of ourselves. Let's take a step back, and we'll give you an overview of XML before showing you the nuts and bolts of applying XML to solve a real business problem.

XML: In the Beginning

Think for a moment: How would you share legal documents among various computer systems so users can retrieve and reformat the documents easily? This can be tricky to accomplish because legal documents aren't like a stack of order forms, where each form has the same kind of information (i.e., customer number, product number) that can be stored in a database. Legal documents have similarities but the text in these documents differs.

This was the problem IBM faced in 1969 when one of their research teams set out to develop a way to integrate information used in law offices. Charles Goldfarb, Ed Losher, and Ray Lorie were members of the team that came up with a solution—Generalized Markup Language (GML). GML consisted of words that described pieces of a legal document.

Although the text in one legal document differs from that in another legal document, legal documents are organized into specific sections. GML was used to identify each section, making it relatively easy for an information system to store and retrieve a section of a legal document.

In 1974, Goldfarb transformed GML into a new all-purpose markup language called Standard Generalized Markup Language (SGML), which the International Organization for Standardization (ISO) eventually adopted in 1986 as a recognized standard used in electronic publishing.

SGML had one major drawback: It was considered too complex. Tim Berners-Lee and Anders Berglund set out to simplify SGML so that it could readily be used to share technical documents over the Internet. Their solution: HTML. HTML consists of a limit set of standard tags that describes how information is to be displayed.

It is this capability that gives HTML its strength—and its weakness. Applications that can read HTML tags can display an HTML document without having to know anything about the document. This differs from a database application that needs to know everything about each data element in the document, such as data type and size, in order to display the data.

However, HTML doesn't describe the data and there's no way for you to enhance the HTML set to describe data. This is the primary weakness of HTML. For example, you can use HTML tags to specify how a book title is displayed, but you cannot use them to identify text as a book title.

It wasn't until 1998, when the World Wide Web Consortium (W3C) agreed to a new standard—XML, that this problem was solved. XML, a subset of SGML, is used to develop a customizable markup language that is as simple to use as HTML and that works with HTML.

As you'll see throughout this book, you'll be able to define your own set of XML tags that describes information that's relative to your business. Furthermore, you'll be able to use HTML to tell the browser—and other applications that can read HTML—how to display that information.

What Is XML?

In a nutshell, XML is a markup language that's used to represent data so data can be easily shared among different kinds of applications that run on different operating systems. To appreciate this, let's take a look at how data is exchanged without XML.

Let's say that you have a hot new web site that sells books. Your site displays the book's ISBN, or International Standard Book Number (the unique number that identifies a book from other books), title, author, table of contents, and other kinds of information that you normally find on a bookseller's web site. All this information is stored in a database and is inserted into a dynamic web page whenever a visitor inquires about the book.

Book information is stored in one or more database tables. A table is similar to a spreadsheet in that it has columns and rows (see Table 1-1). Columns represent a particular kind of data. That is, all book titles appear in the same column and all author names appear in a different column. Each kind of data has its own column. Rows represent books. That is, each row has one ISBN, book title, the author(s), one table of contents, and so on.

ISBN	Title	Author	Table of Contents
0072254548	Java Demystified	Jim Keogh	Chapter 1 Chapter 2 Chapter 3 Chapter 4 Chapter 5
0072253592	Data Structures Demystified	Jim Keogh and Ken Davidson	Chapter 1 Chapter 2 Chapter 3 Chapter 4 Chapter 5

Table 1-1 A Table of Data About a Book That Is Stored in a Database

Columns are described in a variety of ways, depending on the nature of the application and the design of the database. For example, typically, the minimum description for a column in a table that contains information about books includes

- Column name
- Column type (text, numeric, Boolean)
- Maximum size (maximum number of characters that can be stored in the column)

However, some database designers might also describe columns as having a

- Minimum size (minimum number of characters that can be stored in the column)
- Label (text that appears alongside the data when the data is displayed or printed)
- Validation rules (criteria the data must meet before being inserted into the column)
- Formatting (such as the use of hyphens in a Social Security Number)

The list of ways to describe a column seems endless. In order for the data from one application to be shared with another application, this application must be able to understand how each column is described. For example, it must know that the ISBN is text and not a numeric value although an ISBN contains numbers. Otherwise, it might not interpret the data properly.

Furthermore, the application receiving data must know that the ISBN number comes before the title, and the title comes before the author, and the author comes before the table of contents, and so on. Otherwise the application might treat the ISBN number as the author.

Before any data can be exchanged, the developer of the application receiving data must obtain this description of the data and modify the app to read the data. This is time-consuming and complex.

XML makes sharing data at lot easier by enabling a company or, in many cases, an industry to define a standard set of markup tags that describe data. These markup tags are then combined with data to form an XML document, which is then made available to other applications.

These applications reference a known set of tags in order to extract data from the XML document. There is no need to exchange data descriptions because the set of markup tags already describes data in the XML document.

Let's return to our online bookstore example to see how this works. Suppose the book industry agrees on a standard set of markup tags to describe a book. The book publisher creates an XML document that uses these markup tags to describe each of the publisher's books. The XML document is then distributed to retailers and others who require information about a publisher's line of books.

Here is a very simple version of such an XML document. You probably have no trouble understanding this document because the XML tags clearly describe the data. The XML tags are similar in appearance to HTML tags in that there is an open tag (<books>) and a closed tag (</books>). However, unlike HTML, we made up the tag name.

```
<books>
  <book>
    <isbn>0072254548</isbn>
    <title>Java Demystified</title>
    <author>Jim Keogh</author>
    <toc>
      Chapter 1
      Chapter 2
      Chapter 3
      Chapter 4
      Chapter 5
    </toc>
  </book>
  <book>
    <isbn>0072253592</isbn>
    <title>Data Structures Demystified</title>
    <author>Jim Keogh and Ken Davidson </author>
    <toc>
      Chapter 1
      Chapter 2
      Chapter 3
      Chapter 4
      Chapter 5
    </toc>
  </book>
</books>
```

Typically an XML document contains nested elements, which implies the relationship one tag has to other tags in the XML document. In the previous example, the tag <books> contains information about all books. The tag <book> contains information about one particular book, which is identified by other tags, such as <isbn>, <title>, <author>, and <toc>.

The tag <books> is said to be the parent of <book>, and <book> is said to be the parent of <isbn>, <title>, <author>, and <toc>.

Why Is XML Such a Big Deal?

Flexibility. XML enables you to update the definition of the XML document without breaking existing processes—that is, you can make the update without having to alter the application that processes the data.

Let's say that in addition to the ISBN, title, author, and table of content, you want to include the book's publication date. The existing application looks for the original four fields (ISBN, title, author, and table of content) to parse. *Parsing* is the process of stripping out XML tags, leaving only the data left. You can add a fifth field (publication date) without having to break the existing parsing process because each field is delimited with XML markup tags.

In a fixed-length database, the process expects each field to be positioned at a specific location in each row. Inserting a new field might change the location of existing fields, requiring the process to be changed.

XML, however, isn't constrained by a fixed-length data because the size of the data is determined by the location of the XML closed markup tag. Here's how the title can be shown in an XML document:

```
<title>
   XML Demystified: The Greatest Book Ever Printed
</title>
```

You can insert as many characters as you need in the title without affecting applications that share this XML document because they know that the title ends right before the </title> markup tag appears in the XML document, regardless of the length of the title.

Document Type Definitions

Before an application can read an XML document, it must learn what XML markup tags the document uses. It does this by reviewing the document type definition (DTD). The DTD identifies markup tags that can be used in an XML document and defines the structure of those tags in the XML document.

The application that uses the books XML document reads the DTD to learn about each element in the document. It's important to remember that the DTD identifies the name of an XML markup tag and whether or not the tag is a *parent* (contains other tags) or a *child* (contains data). The DTD doesn't tell the application what kind of data it is. That is, it says, "The <isbn> tag is valid." It doesn't say, "The <isbn> tag contains the identifier that uniquely identifies a book."

In some cases, the DTD can also tell the application what values to expect in certain tags. Let's say that the book element has an attribute called format. The default format is Portable Document Format (PDF) and the allowable formats are values Excel spreadsheet (XLS), PDF, plain (ASCII) text file (TXT), Word document (DOC).

The parser returns PDF when you query that attribute if the attribute isn't present in the XML document. If the attribute is present in the XML document, the parser validates that the attribute is one of the four allowable values. You'll learn more about how this works later in Chapter 7. For now, here's how the attribute is written in the DTD:

```
<!ENTITY % book_format "(XLS|PDF|TXT|DOC)">
<!ATTLIST book
format  %book_format; "PDF">
```

For example, the DTD doesn't tell the application what an isbn is. It simply states that isbn is a valid XML tag for this XML document. The developer of the application must build into the application logic to identify and process an isbn. This comes about when companies, vendors, and those in an industry establish a standard XML markup tag set.

Let's return to the books XML document to so you can see the relationship between a DTD and an XML document. The books XML document contains the following markup tags:

<books>
<book>
<isbn>
<title>
<author>
<toc>

The structure is the placement of the markup tags within the XML document. In our example, the <book> markup tag is placed within the <books> markup tag. Likewise, the <isbn>, <title>, <author>, and <toc> markup tags are placed within the <book> markup tag (in that order).

We need to create a DTD that declares these markup tags and shows their relationships. Here's what the DTD looks like.

```
<?xml version="1.0"?>
<!ELEMENT books (book*)>
<!ELEMENT book (isbn, title, author, toc)>
<!ELEMENT isbn (#PCDATA)>
<!ELEMENT title (#PCDATA)>
<!ELEMENT author (#PCDATA)>
<!ELEMENT toc (#PCDATA)>
```

The first line specifies the version of XML that's used to create the XML document. Below this line are statements that declare elements that are used in the XML document. An element is a markup tag. There are three parts to an element declaration.

- First is !ELEMENT, which says that the declaration follows.
- Second is the element name as it appears in the XML document.
- Third is the type of element it is, which is either a group of elements or a Parsed Character Data (PCDATA) element. PCDATA elements cannot contain other elements. Another allowable type is Character Data (CDATA).

The first element that's declared is books. This is a group of elements, so you must list the names of the elements that are members of the group, which is book. The element name book is followed by an asterisk, which means there are zero to many book elements under books. The other allowable qualifiers are

- **?** Zero or one of these (also referred to as a optional tag)
- **+** One to many
- **No qualifier** Exactly one of these

The second element is book, which, too, is a group of elements. Therefore, those elements must be listed when you declare book.

The remaining elements are PCDATA elements and they don't contain other elements.

Where to Place the DTD

The DTD is placed either at the top of the XML document or in a separate file. Begin by placing the DTD at the top of the books XML document, as shown here:

```
<?xml version="1.0"?>
<!DOCTYPE books [
  <!ELEMENT books    (book*)>
  <!ELEMENT book     (isbn, title, author, toc)>
  <!ELEMENT isbn     (#PCDATA)>
  <!ELEMENT title    (#PCDATA)>
  <!ELEMENT author   (#PCDATA)>
  <!ELEMENT toc      (#PCDATA)>
]>
<books>
```

```
  <book>
    <isbn>0072254548</isbn>
    <title>Java Demystified</title>
    <author>Jim Keogh</author>
    <toc>
      Chapter 1
      Chapter 2
      Chapter 3
      Chapter 4
      Chapter 5
    </toc>
  </book>
  <book>
    <isbn>0072253592</isbn>
    <title>Data Structures Demystified</title>
    <author>Jim Keogh and Ken Davidson </author>
    <toc>
      Chapter 1
      Chapter 2
      Chapter 3
      Chapter 4
      Chapter 5
    </toc>
  </book>
</books>
```

Placing the DTD at the top of an XML document is fine if only one XML document uses the DTD. However, this is a problem if multiple XML documents use the same DTD because you'll need to change each XML document whenever the DTD is updated.

A preferred approach is to use an external file that contains the DTD and then reference that file in each XML document that needs to access the DTD. Here's how this works.

First write the DTD and save it to a text file that has the file extension .dtd. We'll call this file books.dtd.

```
<?xml version="1.0"?>
<!ELEMENT books (book)>
<!ELEMENT book (isbn, title, author, toc)>
<!ELEMENT isbn (#PCDATA)>
<!ELEMENT title (#PCDATA)>
<!ELEMENT author (#PCDATA)>
<!ELEMENT toc (#PCDATA)>
```

Next, reference the DTD file at the beginning of the XML document. You do this by specifying the DOCTYPE as we show in this next example. Make sure that you replace the word "books" as the DOCTYPE and "books.dtd" as the file name with an appropriate name for your XML document.

```
<?xml version="1.0"?>
<!DOCTYPE books SYSTEM "books.dtd">
<books>
  <book>
    <isbn>0072254548</isbn>
    <title>Java Demystified</title>
    <author>Jim Keogh</author>
    <toc>
      Chapter 1
      Chapter 2
      Chapter 3
      Chapter 4
      Chapter 5
    </toc>
  </book>
  <book>
    <isbn>0072253592</isbn>
    <title>Data Structures Demystified</title>
    <author>Jim Keogh and Ken Davidson </author>
    <toc>
      Chapter 1
      Chapter 2
      Chapter 3
      Chapter 4
      Chapter 5
    </toc>
  </book>
</books>
```

Reading an XML Document

Information contained in an XML document can be extracted from the document through a process called *parsing*. Parsing is an orderly method of stripping away the XML markup tags leaving only the data. The data is then processed by an application depending on the nature of the application. The program that performs parsing is called a *parser*.

For example, you'd use a parser to retrieve book information from the books XML document that you saw earlier in this chapter. The extracted book information is then combined with HTML code to create a dynamic web page that displays the information about the book on the screen.

Developers use one of two basic parsers. These are the Document Object Model (DOM) parser and the Simple API for XML (SAX).

DOM reads the entire XML document into memory and then creates a tree structure of elements (see Figure 1-1). Various techniques are used to traverse the tree to local information contained in the XML document. You can also use DOM to write data to the XML document, but it's limited to working with small XML documents because the entire XML document is placed in memory.

SAX reads the XML document, noting the locations of markup tags. The SAX parser makes a one-time pass through the XML from start to finish. As it encounters tags and data, it calls events that you define in your code. SAX is ideal for reading large XML documents because there aren't any memory constraints; only a chunk of the XML document is ever in memory at one time. A drawback of SAX is that it cannot traverse an XML document. That is, SAX makes one pass through the document. If you want to return to a previous part of the document, then the document needs to be read from the beginning of the documents.

Both DOM and SAX validate the contents of an XML document against a DTD. You'll learn more about DOM and SAX later in this book.

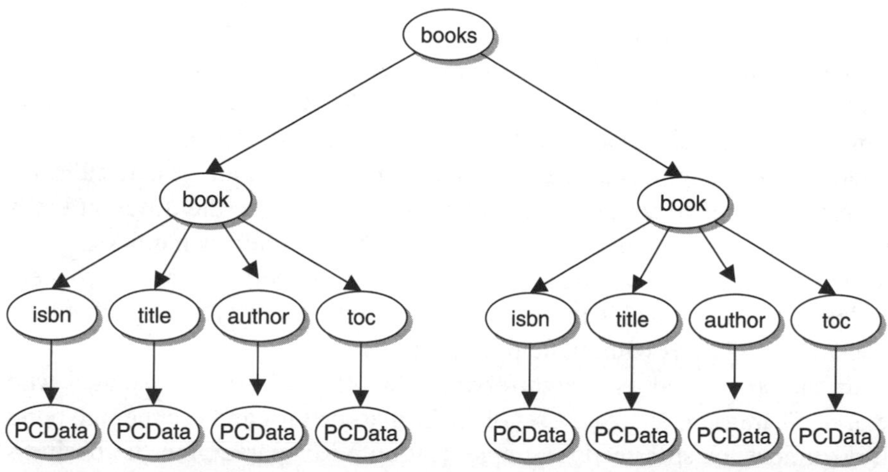

Figure 1-1 DOM transforms elements of an XML document into a tree structure, enabling the parser to traverse elements.

Why Are Corporations Switching to XML?

XML makes exchanging data easy while providing an efficient way to modify an XML document without having to change existing parsing routines. Companies can exchange data with business partners without having to have their IT departments set up elaborate routines to exchange data. This ultimately reduces the cost of doing business.

Prior to XML, corporate IT departments exchanged details of their data formats with their business partners. Programmers then either wrote new programs or modified existing programs to read and process the data.

Before XML took hold, IT departments stored data in databases that use fixed-length rows, which are still widely used today. As you'll recall from earlier in this chapter, a row might contain data about one book. A fixed-length row means that the same space is allocated for every book.

With XML, fields can be inserted into and removed from an XML document without altering the parsing process. This saves the expense that incurred when IT professionals had to modify a process every time a column was added to or removed from a fixed-length database.

It's easy to find data in a database that uses fixed-length rows, especially compared to the effort it takes to parse data in an XML document. It takes more computer power to parse an XML document than it does to find the same data stored in a fixed-length database, because the parser must compare strings of text, evaluate XML markup tags, and validate the structure of the XML document. These tasks aren't necessary to find data in a fixed-length database.

This is the very reason why IT departments initially frown upon switching from a fixed-length database to an XML document. It doesn't make sense for a corporation to move from a very efficient database tool to one that is less efficient.

However, a fixed-length database isn't without its disadvantages. It calls for skilled IT professionals to create and maintain it. Furthermore, the different kinds of fixed-length database products on the market each have their own quirks.

In addition, many business managers have difficulty understanding the concept of a fixed-length database, which makes it challenging to apply database technology to solve business problems without help from IT.

XML, on the other hand, is straightforward, enabling a business manager who has little or no IT training to create a set of XML markup tags and use them to build an XML document. IT still needs to implement an XML parser, but the business manager usually has the skills to apply XML to solve a business problem. Furthermore, more powerful computers are available today at a reasonable cost, thereby overcoming one of the major disadvantages of using XML: the expense.

Web Services

Businesses and their business partners are forever seeking ways to efficiently do business with one another. One of those ways is through exchanging information electronically. For example, it's more efficient to place an order electronically than it is to do it manually. That is, it's faster to have computers talk to computers.

There can be a formidable challenge, though. Both computers must agree on how to exchange the information. Traditionally, this has required that IT people from both companies devise and implement a plan to bring about the exchange.

However, companies are automating this process by using *web services*. Web services are a web of services and have practically nothing to do with the Internet except as a means to exchange information. For example, a supplier might offer a service that accepts orders electronically from customers. This service uses the Internet to transfer the order from the customer to the supplier.

XML is used to send requests and receive replies. It's the best choice for exchanging data because it works with every operating system and programming language.

Looking Ahead

XML is a markup language similar to HTML except that it enables you to create your own tag set. That is, you can use XML to create your own markup language. The most significant difference between HTML and XML is that HTML markup tags are used to describe how information will be displayed while XML markup tags identify the information.

Many companies use XML as a way to exchange data within an organization and among business partners. In order to make this exchange successful, companies and some industries have agreed upon a standard set of XML markup tags to describe data.

Data is stored in an XML document, which is a text file that contains data and markup tags describing the data. An application accesses the data contained in an XML document by parsing the document. Parsing strips away markup tags leaving data, which the application then processes further.

However, before an application reads the XML document, it must learn about the XML markup tags contained in the document by reviewing the document type definition (DTD). The DTD identifies markup tags that can be used in the XML document and defines the structure of these tags.

The DTD can be placed at the top of the XML document or in a separate file if the DTD is going to be used by multiple XML documents. Reference is then made to the DTD file at the beginning of each XML document.

Quiz

1. XML cannot be used with HTML.
   a. True
   b. False
2. XML is more advantageous to use than a fixed-length database system because
   a. Today's computers are faster than they have been in years past.
   b. It saves money by reducing IT expenses.
   c. Those without an IT background can easily understand XML.
   d. All of the above.
3. SAX is
   a. A fixed-length database system
   b. An XML database system
   c. A variable-length database system
   d. An XML parser
4. PCDATA is
   a. An XML element that contains other XML elements
   b. An XML element that contains parsed character data
   c. An XML element that's used to define data for use only on a PC
   d. None of the above
5. The Document Object Model
   a. Defines the layout of an XML document
   b. Defines XML elements that are used in an XML document
   c. Is an XML parser
   d. Is an XML document that contains labels, buttons, and other Graphical User Interface objects
6. You must use a parser to read an XML document.
   a. True
   b. False

7. XML stores data in fixed lengths.
   a. True
   b. False
8. XML is a subset of
   a. SGML
   b. HTML
   c. MGL
   d. None of the above
9. XML is used for web services.
   a. True
   b. False
10. An XML element can contain other XML elements.
   a. True
   b. False

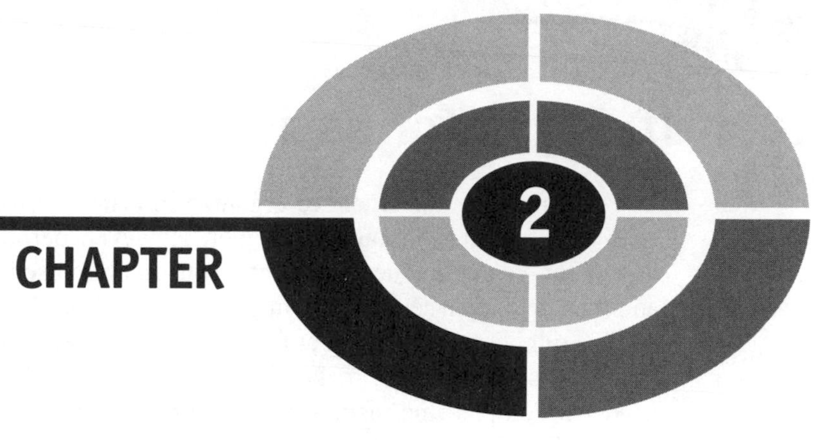

Creating an XML Document

Now that you have an understanding of what XML is and how it works, it's time to learn how to apply your knowledge and design your own set of XML markup tags, and then use those tags to write your first XML document.

Creating a set of XML markup tags requires you to analyze and organize the information that you want to place in an XML document. You'll need to find the natural relationships within pieces of information so you can describe those relationships in your document type definition.

In this chapter, you'll learn step-by-step how to do this, along with other design features, to build a working XML document that enables you to share information electronically among various applications.

Identifying Information

You use an XML document to organize information from a business transaction, such as information about a customer. However, before you can create an XML document, you'll first need to identify information used in the business transaction and then develop a set of XML markup tags to describe this information.

This might seem daunting at first, but it isn't if you carefully review each step in the business transaction, making sure that you identify each piece of information needed to complete the business transaction. Don't be concerned if all the information you find isn't used in an XML document. At this point, simply identify the information. Later, you'll decide if you should include it in the XML document.

Let's walk through an example of an order transaction and identify customer information by first listing the steps in the transaction. List these steps in the order they're performed. For more complex transactions, you may want to draw a flowchart that illustrates each step in the transaction. We'll keep the transaction simple in this example. Here are the steps in the order transaction:

1. The customer selects products.
2. The customer checks out.
3. The customer is prompted to enter an account number.
4. If the customer does not enter an account number, then the customer is prompted to open an account.
5. If the customer decides to open an account, the customer is prompted to enter personal information and is then returned to the checkout process.
6. The customer is presented with the subtotal for the purchase.
7. The customer is prompted to select a shipping method.
8. Shipping charges are calculated and added to the subtotal, which is then presented to the customer.
9. The customer is prompted to select a billing method.
10. The customer is then asked to confirm the order, and with positive confirmation, the order is processed.

Noticed that we've described the transaction in sufficient detail to identify the information used in the transaction, but not at the level of detail necessary to program the application.

Review the steps of this transaction and focus in on those ones that contain customer information, such as the step where the customer opens a new account.

Review any documentation, such as that for a new account, which describes the information required to open this account.

Here's a list of the information that's needed to open a new account:

- First Name
- Last Name
- Title
- Company
- Street Address 1
- Street Address 2
- City
- State
- Zip
- Business Phone
- Cell Phone
- Home Phone
- Fax
- E-mail
- Account Number

Creating XML Markup Tags

Practically any word can be used as an XML markup tag so long as it isn't a reserved XML word, such as <?xml>, which is a processing instruction. The element tag cannot contain any white space. In places where white space makes it easier to read, such as "first name," an underscore is typically used: "first_name." XML parsers are case sensitive so "first_name" is not equal to "First_Name." The common convention is to use all lowercase letters as it makes it less confusing for the programmers parsing the XML. The word should describe the information. Many times you can use the label you'll use on the order form to describe the information for the XML markup tag. For example, a new account form will have First Name as a label. It makes sense to use this as the XML markup tag for the customer's first name.

Be sure that the XML markup tag explicitly describes the information and is not so general that the tag could be misconstrued. Suppose the new account form has a label First Name, which describes the customer first name. You're going to nest it inside the customer element so there is no ambiguity. The names should be as short and concise as possible.

As you learned in the previous chapter, XML markup tags are organized into a parent/child relationship where a parent XML markup tag contains children markup tags. A child markup tag contains information. Looking at this from the parser perspective, a markup tag is almost always a parent; the child is the text (otherwise referred to as an *element node* and a *text node*).

Identifying a parent/child relationship is intuitive in most cases. Think of a parent as an object such as an order form, invoice, credit notice, and customer. Children are information that are contained within the parent, such as a customer's first name and city. For example, Customer is a likely name for a parent because it contains XML markup tags representing customer information. Make a list of these objects using indenting to show the relationship between a parent and its children, as we've illustrated here:

```
customer
   first_name
   last_name
   title
   company
   street_1
   street_2
   city
   state
   zip
   business_phone
   cell_phone
   home_phone
   fax
   email
   account_number
```

Parent ... Parent/Child ... Child

Sometimes it makes sense to further organize XML markup tags into a parent ... parent/child ... child relationship where the child of a parent is also a parent, as we illustrate in the following diagram:

```
Parent
   Parent/Child
      Child
```

Let's see how this applies to our customer information example. Look over the customer information and try to find subgroups of information. You'll probably notice customer name, customer address, and customer phone number as three natural groups. These make good parent/child candidates.

Each parent/child must have its own XML markup tag so that an application can retrieve its children. Suppose, for example, that an application wants the customer's mailing address. The application can grab the customer address parent, then parse the child elements to get the various parts of the address.

This new set of XML markup tags reflects the parent/child element:

```
customer
   name
      first_name
      last_name
   title
   company
   address
      street_1
      street_2
      city
      state
      zip
   phone
      business
      cell
      home
      fax
   email
   account_number
```

Our list of XML markup tags is almost complete; however, one tag is missing. These tags define information for one customer, yet multiple customers will appear in the XML document. Furthermore, the XML document will likely contain other information in addition to customer information.

Therefore, it makes sense to organize the XML document into sections, one of which is customers. A section is simply another parent/child element as shown here:

```
customers
   customer
      name
         first_name
         last_name
      title
      company
      address
```

```
        street_1
        street_2
        city
        state
        zip
    phone
        business
        cell
        home
        fax
    email
    account_number
```

Creating a Document Type Definition

After you create a set of XML markup tags, the next step is to create a document type definition (DTD). A DTD identifies the markup tags that can be used in an XML document and it defines the structure of those tags, which you learned about in the previous chapter. The DTD identifies the name of the XML markup tag and whether or not the tag is a parent or child.

Here's the DTD for the customer information example:

```
<?xml version="1.0"?>
   <!ELEMENT customers (customer*)>
   <!ELEMENT customer (name, title, company,
         address, phone, email, account_number)>
   <!ELEMENT name (first_name, last_name)>
   <!ELEMENT address (street_1, street_2, city, state, zip)>
   <!ELEMENT phone (business, cell, home, fax)>
   <!ELEMENT first_name (#PCDATA)>
   <!ELEMENT last_name (#PCDATA)>
   <!ELEMENT title (#PCDATA)>
   <!ELEMENT company (#PCDATA)>
   <!ELEMENT street_1 (#PCDATA)>
   <!ELEMENT street_2 (#PCDATA)>
   <!ELEMENT city (#PCDATA)>
   <!ELEMENT state (#PCDATA)>
   <!ELEMENT zip (#PCDATA)>
   <!ELEMENT business (#PCDATA)>
   <!ELEMENT cell (#PCDATA)>
   <!ELEMENT home (#PCDATA)>
   <!ELEMENT fax (#PCDATA)>
   <!ELEMENT email (#PCDATA)>
   <!ELEMENT account_number (#PCDATA)>
```

This DTD has two types of elements—parent and child. Let's examine the second line of the DTD, which describes the first element, customers. Customers is a parent element and it contains the child element, customer. Notice that an asterisk follows customer. The asterisk means there is zero to many customer elements under customers. When you specify child elements, you can use three qualifiers that define the number of occurrences of that child element:

- * Zero to many occurrences
- + One to many occurrences
- ? Zero or one occurrences

The last one is sometimes referred to as the "optional" qualifier since it means either zero or one of the elements will be present. For example, the customer record includes a fax number. If you want this data to be optional in the XML, you could change this line in the DTD:

```
<!ELEMENT phone (business, cell, home, fax)>
```

to:

```
<!ELEMENT phone (business, cell, home, fax?)>
```

This would mean that fax is an optional element nested with the phone element. Since business, cell, and home don't have any qualifiers, they must appear once—and only once—under the phone element. Furthermore, the business, cell, home, and fax elements must appear in exactly the order they're specified in the DTD.

Skip down to the seventh line in the DTD where first_name is defined as containing PCDATA. This, and the remaining lines in the DTD, defines child elements. Each of these child elements contains a child text node. The data in the text node is Parsed Character Data (PCDATA), as designated by the PCDATA tag in the DTD.

Creating an XML Document

The final step is to create the XML document. Begin by placing the DTD at the top of the document, as we show in the next example. An XML parser reads these definitions before parsing elements of the XML document.

Alternatively, you can write the DTD to a text file and then reference the text file at the top of the XML document, as we described in the previous chapter. You could have saved the DTD to the file customers.dtd and then replaced the DOCTYPE and DTD in the next example with the following line:

```
<!DOCTYPE Customers SYSTEM "customers.dtd">
```

When writing the XML document, be sure to enclose each element in angled brackets (< >), and always have an open (<) and closed markup tag (</). You place child elements within the open and closed markup tags of a parent element, and place information within the open and closed markup tags of a child element.

Here's the completed XML document. The first line of the document is a processing instruction that explicitly identifies this document as an XML document. This isn't required, but it's normally included. The DTD comes next, followed by the elements of the XML document.

```
<?xml version="1.0"?>
<!DOCTYPE customers [
   <!ELEMENT customers (customer*)>
   <!ELEMENT customer (name, title, company,
        address, phone, email, account_number)>
   <!ELEMENT name (first_name, last_name)>
   <!ELEMENT address (street_1, street_2, city, state, zip)>
   <!ELEMENT phone (business, cell, home, fax)>
   <!ELEMENT first_name (#PCDATA)>
   <!ELEMENT last_name (#PCDATA)>
   <!ELEMENT title (#PCDATA)>
   <!ELEMENT company (#PCDATA)>
   <!ELEMENT street_1 (#PCDATA)>
   <!ELEMENT street_2 (#PCDATA)>
   <!ELEMENT city (#PCDATA)>
   <!ELEMENT state (#PCDATA)>
   <!ELEMENT zip (#PCDATA)>
   <!ELEMENT business (#PCDATA)>
   <!ELEMENT cell (#PCDATA)>
   <!ELEMENT home (#PCDATA)>
   <!ELEMENT fax (#PCDATA)>
   <!ELEMENT email (#PCDATA)>
   <!ELEMENT account_number (#PCDATA)>
]>
<customers>
   <customer>
      <name>
         <first_name>Bob</first_name>
         <last_name>Smith</last_name>
      </name>
      <title>Manager</title>
      <company>My Company Inc.</company>
      <address>
```

```
            <street_1>The Tech Building</street_1>
            <street_2>555 5th Street</street_2>
            <city>Some City</city>
            <state>NJ</state>
            <zip>07665</zip>
        </address>
        <phone>
            <business>555-555-1212</business>
            <cell>555-555-5432</cell>
            <home>555-555-7678</home>
            <fax>555-555-9989</fax>
        </phone>
        <email>bsmith@mycompany.com</email>
        <account_number>6970654</account_number>
    </customer>
</customers>
```

Attributes

An *attribute* is information that modifies an XML markup tag. You're probably familiar with attributes from when you've used an <img> HTML markup tag to display an image on a web page. The <img> tag tells the browser to display an image. The attribute src tells the browser what image you want to display, as shown here:

```
<img src="image.gif">
```

Attributes work the same way in XML. An attribute is sometimes called a *name/value pair.* The name is the name of the attribute. The value is the value assigned to the attribute. That is, "src" is the attribute's name and "image.gif" is the value assigned to the attribute.

Attributes are placed within the opening markup tag. You can create as many attributes as required, however each attribute must have a unique name, a value contained with quotations; and each name/value pair must be separated by a space. Like element names, attribute names cannot contain whitespace characters. This makes it impossible to parse the XML. The value of an attribute is enclosed in quotations and can contain white space.

XML gives you the flexibility to create your own attributes. That is, you pick the name of the attribute and the attribute's value. This can be tricky because you must be careful not to confuse an attribute with the information that the XML markup tag describes.

Suppose, for example, that you require that the customer ID be stored in the XML document. There are at least two ways to do this. First, you could create a customer ID child tag within the customer parent tag:

```
<cust_id>
```

The other way is to place the customer ID in an attribute of the customer tag, as shown here:

```
<customer cust_id="12345">
```

Some developers prefer using an attribute to store a unique identifier for a parent that represents a single instance such as a customer, order, or product because the attribute makes it easier to identify each instance within the XML document. We illustrate this in the following example, which contains two instances of a customer. Notice that the customer ID pops out at you when you're scanning these XML markup tags. Generally it's best to use attributes when you have a value that's unique to that element as a whole and is unlikely to change. In other words, you're always going to have one, and only one, cust_id for a customer, but you can have several addresses (tomorrow you decide to add mailing, billing, and delivery addresses), many phone numbers, etc. Whether you've used attributes or XML markup tags, the parser is able to extract the customer ID from the XML document.

```
<customers>
<customer cust_id="12345">
   <name>
      <first_name>Bob</first_name>
      <last_name>Smith</last_name>
   </name>
   <title>Manager</title>
   <company>My Company Inc.</company>
</customer>
<customer ID="56789">
   <name>
      <first_name>Tom</first_name>
      <last_name>Jones</last_name>
   </name>
   <title>Vice President</title>
   <company>His Company Inc.</company>
</customer>
</customers>
```

Comments

A *comment* is information in the XML document that's typically not part of the actual data. For example, if you're transferring an XML data file to another company, you may put a comment that gives your name, address, phone, and the date/time that the transfer occurred. If you have a large document and need to split it into multiple smaller documents, you might put a sequence number in the comments. The information in the comments is often data that can be determined from the XML, but having comments makes it easier to troubleshoot and keeps records.

A comment doesn't need to be declared in the DTD. One of the features of an XML parser is you can tell it whether or not to ignore comments. Since comments are not usually part of the data, it's most common to ignore them while processing the document.

You insert a comment into an XML document the same way you insert one into an HTML document. That is, you use the open comment (<!--) and close comment (-->). The parser considers any characters between the open and closed comments a comment. The only sequence of characters not permitted between the opening and closing tags is "- -." The parser uses this special sequence to find the closing tag.

A comment can be placed on a single line or multiple lines, as shown here:

```
<customer cust_id="12345">
   <!-- File sent at 10:35 EST -->
   <name>
      <first_name>Bob</first_name>
      <last_name>Smith</last_name>
   </name>
   <!--
       Valid Titles
       President
       Vice President
       Manager
    -->
   <title>Manager</title>
   <company>My Company Inc.</company>
</customer>
```

Entities

Although XML has few special characters, there are enough that conflict with information that's contained in the XML document. Let's say that your XML document contains a formula, as shown here. You probably don't have any problem reading it. The formula simply says "a < b."

```
<formula>a<b</formula>
```

However, this formula will confuse the parser and cause an error to occur because the "<" is an XML special character that tells the parser that the characters following the "<" are an XML markup tag.

You can avoid such confusion by using entities in place of characters that conflict with XML special characters. An *entity* is a name preceded by an ampersand (&) that tells the parser that you want to use XML special characters as information—and not as XML tags. Table 2-1 contains commonly used entities.

Here's the correct way to write the formula in an XML document:

```
<formula>a&lt;b</formula>
```

Some documents contain unusual characters, especially those that have scientific or mathematical formulas. For example, you probably have seen this one in your geometry book: π. This is the symbol for pi. You won't find this symbol on your keyboard. In order to insert this symbol into an XML document, you'll need to refer to its UNICODE value.

UNICODE is a standard that associates a numeric value to characters that are used in documents. Every character on your keyboard has a UNICODE value. Likewise, every character in nearly every language spoken around the world has a UNICODE value. You can look up UNICODE in your favorite search engine to see the value that's associated with the character you want to insert into your XML document.

XML Keyword	Entity
<	<
>	>
"	"
'	'
&	&

Table 2-1 Use the Entity Whenever Information Takes the Form of an XML Keyword

You insert the UNICODE value into your XML document by using the ampersand, and then the pound symbol followed by the number. Here's how you'd insert the π symbol into your XML document:

```
<PI>&#227;</PI>
```

In the customers XML document example, the DTD specifies that the child elements contain PCDATA; for example:

```
<!ELEMENT first_name (#PCDATA)>
```

This means that the data between the opening and closing first_name tags can contain this special character entity, as we described above. This is what is meant by *parsed* character data. If the parser sees "<," it recognizes this as a special entity: the return "<" to the application processing the XML. Similarly, if the application is building the XML document and tells the parser to put "<" as a piece of data, the parser recognizes this special entity and puts "<" into the document. The other option is Character Data (CDATA). If you specify the data between the tags as CDATA, then no special entities are allowed. Trying to put a "<" in the data results in an error.

Processing Instructions

A *processing instruction* is a command that you give to the application that's going to use the information contained in the XML document. For example, you might say, "Only process new customers." The actual commands that you use depends on the commands the application that is processing your XML document recognizes.

If you're writing the XML document and the application that processes the XML document, then you can create your own commands for processing the document. However, for existing applications, you'll have to use commands that the person who wrote the application has defined.

A processing instruction is not part of the data in an XML document. Instead, the parser passes along a processing instruction to the application. Here's how to insert a processing instruction into your XML document. Processing instructions that start with "xml" are reserved for current and future standards.

```
<?command?>
```

CDATA Sections

The CDATA section is part of an XML document that contains only data, and doesn't contain XML markup tags. The parser passes data contained in this section to the application that is using the XML document.

The CDATA section is defined as:

```
<![CDATA["12345" "98765"]]>
```

The section opens with <![CDATA[and ends with]]>. Data appears between them. The data between the tags is passed to the application without any translation or interpretation. In this case,

```
"12345" "98765"
```

would be passed to the application as a raw string. One of the more common uses of a CDATA section is to pass binary data in XML, such as an image file. A CDATA section may appear anywhere in an XML document where character data appears.

Looking Ahead

In order to create an XML document, you must first develop a set of XML markup tags by analyzing the information you want included in that document. During the analysis, you'll need to identify the natural organization of the information in terms of parent ... child and parent ... child/parent ...child relationship.

The next step is to create the document type definition (DTD) so that the parser knows which XML markup tags are valid for the XML document. You can store the DTD at the top of the document or in a text file, which is then referenced at the top of the document. Next, you'll use the XML markup tags that you created and write your XML document.

An XML markup tag can contain one or more attributes. Attributes are name/value pairs that contain information that modifies the tag. However, some developers use attributes to store information, such as a customer ID, which can be included as its own XML markup tag.

Comments are used to place reminders throughout the XML document. The parser usually ignores them and they're not passed along to the application that's using the XML document.

Sometimes conflicts arise between an XML special character and a character entered as part of the information of a markup tag. An entity resolves these conflicts. It's a symbol used in the XML document that replaces the conflicting character.

You can include processing instructions in an XML document to instruct the application that uses the XML application on how to process the application. The parser passes along processing instructions to the application.

The CDATA section of an XML document is a collection of data without tags that's passed to the application.

Quiz

1. A parent element cannot contain another parent element.
    a. True
    b. False
2. An attribute contains a
    a. Name/value pair
    b. Value/name pair
    c. The data section of the XML document
    d. None of the above
3. The asterisk at the end of an element name in a DTD means it's
    a. The end of the list of elements
    b. The beginning of the list of elements
    c. The DTD contains zero to many of this element
    d. The DTD contains this element and fewer elements
4. What does the parser do with the CDATA section of an XML document?
    a. Ignores it
    b. Passes the data to the application that uses the XML document without any translation or interpretation
    c. Deletes the data before passing the XML document to the application that uses the XML document
    d. None of the above
5. The DOCTYPE is used to
    a. Create the CDATA section of an XML document
    b. Create an XML document
    c. Identify the DTD for an XML document
    d. Identify the parser that is used to parse the XML document
6. A child element can be a parent element.
    a. True
    b. False

7. All XML markup tags must have an attribute.
   a. True
   b. False
8. Special symbols can be inserted into an XML document using
   a. CDATA
   b. A UNICODE value
   c. An attribute
   d. A comment
9. You avoid conflict between an XML special character and information in an XML document by using a comment.
   a. True
   b. False
10. A processing command is removed from an XML document before the XML document is passed along to the application that uses the XML document.
    a. True
    b. False

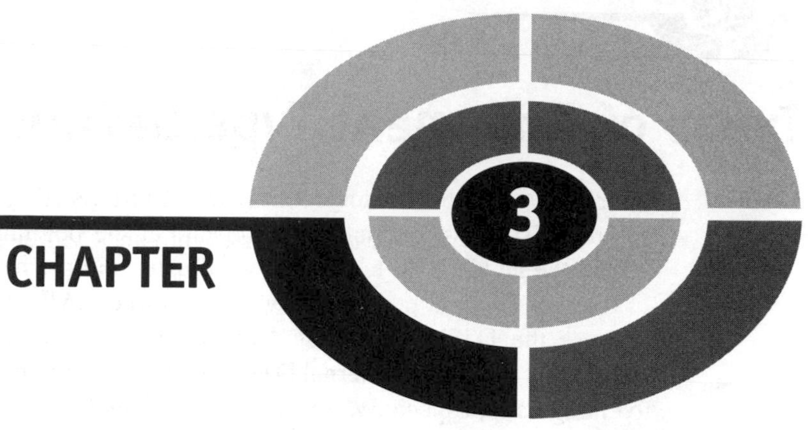

Document Type Definitions

Throughout this book you've learned that you create an XML document using a set of markup tags much like you use for an HTML document. However, markup tags used in an XML document usually conform to a standard set of markup tags that are adopted by a company or an industry rather than the single standard used for all HTML documents.

An *XML standard* is defined in a document type definition (DTD) that specifies the markup tags that can be used in the XML document along with the parent-child structure of those tags. The *XML parser* uses the DTD as reference when parsing elements of the XML document.

We've introduced you to the basic concept of a DTD in the last chapter. Now we'll take an in-depth look at how to develop your own DTD and explore features XML developers commonly use.

Types of Document Type Definition

There are two types of document type definitions (DTD): an *internal DTD* and an *external DTD*. An internal DTD appears at the beginning of the XML document within the DOCTYPE tag, which we illustrate in the next example.

Internal DTD is perfect for when only one XML document will use the DTD because the DTD is distributed in the same file as the XML document. Some developers also use an internal DTD for small documents where the DTD is unlikely to change and, especially, for those documents that will only be distributed within their organization.

Avoid using an internal DTD if many XML documents share the same DTD because it isn't economical to replicate the DTD in every XML document. Furthermore, you'll need to hunt down each of those documents whenever you want to change the DTD.

Notice that the following example uses an internal DTD to define a customer for the XML document. This DTD contains a number of parent-child relationships (see Chapter 2), as you can tell from reading the definition of the customer tag.

The customer tag is a parent than contains seven child elements. These are name, title, company, address, phone, email, and account_number. Three of those child elements are also parents to their own child elements.

For example, name has first_name and last_name as child elements. Address has street_1, street_2, city, state, and zip as child elements. And phone has business, cell, home, and fax as child elements.

The DTD ends with]>. The XML document begins on the next line, where tags defined in the DTD identify data within the XML document.

```
<?xml version="1.0"?>
<!DOCTYPE customers [
   <!ELEMENT customers (customer*)>
   <!ELEMENT customer (name, title, company,
        address, phone, email, account_number)>
   <!ELEMENT name (first_name, last_name)>
   <!ELEMENT address (street_1, street_2, city, state, zip)>
   <!ELEMENT phone (business, cell, home, fax)>
   <!ELEMENT first_name (#PCDATA)>
   <!ELEMENT last_name (#PCDATA)>
   <!ELEMENT title (#PCDATA)>
   <!ELEMENT company (#PCDATA)>
   <!ELEMENT street_1 (#PCDATA)>
   <!ELEMENT street_2 (#PCDATA)>
```

```
    <!ELEMENT city (#PCDATA)>
    <!ELEMENT state (#PCDATA)>
    <!ELEMENT zip (#PCDATA)>
    <!ELEMENT business (#PCDATA)>
    <!ELEMENT cell (#PCDATA)>
    <!ELEMENT home (#PCDATA)>
    <!ELEMENT fax (#PCDATA)>
    <!ELEMENT email (#PCDATA)>
    <!ELEMENT account_number (#PCDATA)>
]>
<customers>
  <customer>
     <name>
        <first_name>Bob</first_name>
        <last_name>Smith</last_name>
     </name>
      <title>Manager</title>
     <company>My Company Inc.</company>
     <address>
        <street_1>The Tech Building</street_1>
        <street_2>555 5th Street</street_2>
        <city>Some City</city>
        <state>NJ</state>
        <zip>07665</zip>
     </address>
     <phone>
        <business>555-555-1212</business>
        <cell>555-555-5432</cell>
        <home>555-555-7678</home>
        <fax>555-555-9989</fax>
     </phone>
     <email>bsmith@mycompany.com</email>
     <account_number>6970654</account_number>
   </customer>
</customers>
```

External Document Type Definition

The external DTD is a DTD that isn't included in an XML document. Instead, it's placed in its own file that has a .dtd file extension. An external DTD can be shared by any XML document if you reference the DTD at the beginning of the XML document.

Let's convert the internal DTD we showed you in the previous example into an external DTD and then reference the DTD from an XML document. The first step is to copy the DTD into its own file. You can do this using any text editor. We'll call the file customers.dtd. The file name should represent the contents of the file. Here's the customers.dtd file:

```
<!ELEMENT customers (customer*)>
<!ELEMENT customer (name, title, company, address, phone, email, account_number)>
<!ELEMENT name (first_name, last_name)>
<!ELEMENT address (street_1, street_2, city, state, zip)>
<!ELEMENT phone (business, cell, home, fax)>
<!ELEMENT first_name (#PCDATA)>
<!ELEMENT last_name (#PCDATA)>
<!ELEMENT title (#PCDATA)>
<!ELEMENT company (#PCDATA)>
<!ELEMENT street_1 (#PCDATA)>
<!ELEMENT street_2 (#PCDATA)>
<!ELEMENT city (#PCDATA)>
<!ELEMENT state (#PCDATA)>
<!ELEMENT zip (#PCDATA)>
<!ELEMENT business (#PCDATA)>
<!ELEMENT cell (#PCDATA)>
<!ELEMENT home (#PCDATA)>
<!ELEMENT fax (#PCDATA)>
<!ELEMENT email (#PCDATA)>
<!ELEMENT account_number (#PCDATA)>
```

The last step is to reference the external DTD from an XML document. You'll use the same XML document you used for the internal DTD. You reference the external DTD in the DOCTYPE tag by using SYSTEM followed by the external DTD file name within quotations, as we show in the next example.

The parser encounters the reference to the external DTD as soon as it reads the DOCTYPE tag. It reads the external DTD from the customers.dtd file next, and then continues reading the XML document.

```
<?xml version="1.0"?>
<!DOCTYPE customers SYSTEM "customers.dtd">
<customers>
   <customer>
      <name>
         <first_name>Bob</first_name>
         <last_name>Smith</last_name>
      </name>
      <title>Manager</title>
      <company>My Company Inc.</company>
      <address>
         <street_1>The Tech Building</street_1>
         <street_2>555 5th Street</street_2>
         <city>Some City</city>
```

```
        <state>NJ</state>
        <zip>07665</zip>
    </address>
    <phone>
       <business>555-555-1212</business>
       <cell>555-555-5432</cell>
       <home>555-555-7678</home>
       <fax>555-555-9989</fax>
    </phone>
    <email>bsmith@mycompany.com</email>
    <account_number>6970654</account_number>
  </customer>
</customers>
```

External DTD are commonly used when XML documents are exchanged among business partners. Business partners agree to the structure of the DTD and then share the same external DTD for multiple XML documents.

Typically one organization will be the "owner" of the DTD and is responsible for updating it and making it accessible to any partner that's using it. The most common way to share a DTD is to make the source reference a URL. The DTD can be posted on a public web server so anybody using it can reference it. Even though one company or organization controls the DTD, they still need to agree on the content of the XML with their partners.

In one sense, it's good practice to use a DTD so that all parties using it agree and understand the exact structure of the document. Any change to the DTD needs to be clearly communicated. Another good reason to use a DTD is that the XML parsers can validate the structure of the document. There's no need to write a lot of custom code for validation. The parser already has this built in to it. For example, if the parser comes across an element tag in the above document that has <middle_name>, this tag isn't defined in the DTD and the parser throws an error. There is no need to check for this in the application code; the parser checks it for you.

Another feature in the parser is its ability to ignore certain types of white space. Oftentimes an XML document may be structured like this to make it more human readable:

```
<name>
        <first_name>Joe</first_name>
        <last_name>Brown</last_name>
</name>
```

Technically there's a text node between the <name> tag and <first_name> tag. The value (on a Windows platform) is three characters, which consist of a carriage return, line feed, and tab. These characters aren't part of the content of the

document—they're present just to make the XML more human readable. This would be equally valid XML:

```
<name><first_name>Joe</first_name><last_name>Brown</last_name></name>
```

If you're using a DTD, you can tell the parser to "ignore white space." What is white space? It refers to any of the first 33 characters in the ASCII table. This includes the space character, carriage return, line feed, tab, escape, backspace, and several others. The parser looks at the document and recognizes from the DTD that the <name> tag is supposed to be followed by the <first_name> tag. If the only characters between the <name> tag and <first_name> tag are white space (the first 33 characters in the ASCII table), then the parser ignores them.

Shared Document Type Definition

You can use a DTD for a subset of an XML document rather than apply it to the entire document. This is referred to as a *shared DTD*, which shouldn't be confused with an external DTD that's shared by two or more XML documents.

For example, the developer may have a structure for telephone numbers that will be standard for all XML documents that use telephone numbers. The developer could copy the telephone number structure in the DTD for each document. Although this standardizes the structure of the telephone number, there's an inherit problem: The developer must change these DTDs whenever there's a change to the structure of the telephone number.

A more efficient approach is to set up the telephone number structure in a shared DTD and then reference it as a subset of the DTD for the XML document. The shared DTD then becomes an extension to the XML document's DTD.

Here's how this works. First you'll need to create a shared DTD that contains the structure of the telephone number. The shared DTD is an external DTD. That is, the shared DTD is stored in its own file. Consider this snippet of XML:

```
<phone>
   <business>555-555-1212</business>
   <cell>555-555-5432</cell>
   <home>555-555-7678</home>
   <fax>555-555-9989</fax>
</phone>
```

The DTD for this snippet of XML looks like this:

```
<!ELEMENT phone (business,cell,home,fax)>
<!ELEMENT business (#PCDATA)>
<!ELEMENT cell (#PCDATA)>
```

```
<!ELEMENT home (#PCDATA)>
<!ELEMENT fax (#PCDATA)>
```

We'll save this in a file called phone.dtd.

Next, we'll show you how to create an external DTD for the XML document. We'll modify the customers.dtd that we created earlier in the chapter by removing the definition of the phone tag and then inserting reference to the phone.dtd.

Here's the revised customers.dtd. Reference to the phone.dtd appears in the last two lines of the customers.dtd. Notice that this reference is made as an attribute of an ENTITY tag rather than a DOCTYPE tag.

The last line in the DTD—%phone;—defines the ENTITY, and the ENTITY tag identifies where to find the resource "phone.dtd".

```
<!ELEMENT customers (customer*)>
<!ELEMENT customer (name, title, company, address, phone, email, account_number)>
<!ELEMENT name (first_name, last_name)>
<!ELEMENT address (street_1, street_2, city, state, zip)>
<!ELEMENT first_name (#PCDATA)>
<!ELEMENT last_name (#PCDATA)>
<!ELEMENT title (#PCDATA)>
<!ELEMENT company (#PCDATA)>
<!ELEMENT street_1 (#PCDATA)>
<!ELEMENT street_2 (#PCDATA)>
<!ELEMENT city (#PCDATA)>
<!ELEMENT state (#PCDATA)>
<!ELEMENT zip (#PCDATA)>
<!ELEMENT email (#PCDATA)>
<!ELEMENT account_number (#PCDATA)>
<!ENTITY % phone SYSTEM "phone.dtd">
%phone;
```

Here's the XML document that uses the phone tag. This document only needs to reference the customers.dtd and not the phone.dtd because the customers.dtd links to the phone.dtd.

```
<?xml version="1.0"?>
<!DOCTYPE customers SYSTEM "customers.dtd">
<customers>
   <customer>
      <name>
         <first_name>Bob</first_name>
         <last_name>Smith</last_name>
      </name>
      <title>Manager</title>
      <company>My Company Inc.</company>
      <address>
         <street_1>The Tech Building</street_1>
         <street_2>555 5th Street</street_2>
         <city>Some City</city>
```

```
            <state>NJ</state>
            <zip>07665</zip>
        </address>
        <phone>
            <business>555-555-1212</business>
            <cell>555-555-5432</cell>
            <home>555-555-7678</home>
            <fax>555-555-9989</fax>
        </phone>
        <email>bsmith@mycompany.com</email>
        <account_number>6970654</account_number>
    </customer>
</customers>
```

The way organizations can use shared DTDs to create DTD subsets that can be assembled into a DTD for an XML document is similar to how classes can be used in object-oriented programs to build complex objects.

Assembling a DTD from DTD subsets helps speed development while maintaining standards across an organization. For example, a developer whose XML document requires telephone numbers doesn't have to define a phone tag. Instead, the developer references the phone.dtd.

Likewise, the organization doesn't have to worry that DTDs around the company have different definitions for a phone tag because one developer defines the phone tag in the phone.dtd and other developers reference that shared DTD.

Furthermore, changes to a shared DTD occur in one place by one developer, but immediately affect all DTDs that reference that shared DTD. Suppose the organization decides to expand the phone tag definition to include a cell phone. One developer changes the phone.dtd and that change is instantaneously available to the other DTDs. This means an XML document can contain a cell phone number without having to change its DTD.

Element Declarations

An *element* is a portion of the DTD that describes an XML markup tag that can be used in the XML document. It defines an XML markup tag, along with the child of the element. The child may be other elements, character data, or EMPTY. (We'll cover EMPTY later in this chapter.)

An element is declared within the document type definition by using the following form:

```
<!ELEMENT  element_name  ( names of child elements or character data type )>
```

The element_name is the name of the tag, and its child data are placed within the parentheses. Here's the declaration of the customer element, which you used previously in this chapter. The customer element consists of seven child elements.

```
<!ELEMENT customer (name, title, company, address, phone, email, account_number)>
```

An element that contains character data is declared similarly, except #PCDATA is placed between the parentheses. (PCDATA is an acronym for Parsed Character Data.) Here's the way you declare this type of element:

```
<!ELEMENT  element_name  (#PCDATA)>
```

For example, the title element of customer contains character data and is declared as follows:

```
<!ELEMENT title (#PCDATA)>
```

This declaration tells the XML parser that PCDATA is between the opening and closing tags for title:

```
<title>Manager</title>
```

In an XML parser, the basic building blocks of an XML document are referred to as *nodes*. An element is one type of node. In the case of the customer tag, the child nodes are other elements. In the case of the title tag, the child node is referred to as a *text node*. So in the example above, the value of the title child node is "Manager." Every time you define an element, you define the type of child node. It will be other element node(s) or a text node.

Specifying the Number of Occurrences in an Element

You can specify the number of times a child element can be used within a parent element by inserting one of three symbols as the last character in the name of the child element. These symbols are shown in Table 3-1.

Let's say that you declare a customer name as having three child elements, which are first_name, middle_name, and last_name. However, not every customer has a middle name. Therefore, you need to indicate in the declaration that the middle name is optional. Also you want to use only one middle name, should a customer have a middle name(s).

Symbol	Number of Occurrences
*	Zero to many
+	One to many
?	Zero or one

Table 3-1 Symbols Used to Specify the Number of Occurrences of a Child Element Within a Parent Element

XML developers define middle_name as having zero to one occurrence. That is, the customer may have no middle name, or only one middle name but not multiple middle names.

Reviewing Table 3-1, you'll notice that the question mark is the symbol you use to indicate zero to one occurrence. Here's how you write this in the declaration for the middle_name:

```
<!ELEMENT name (first_name, middle_name?, last_name)>
<!ELEMENT first_name (#PCDATA)>
<!ELEMENT middle_name (#PCDATA)>
<!ELEMENT last_name (#PCDATA)>
```

This declaration of the name and the middle_name enables the XML document to contain the following data. You'll notice two customers are entered into this document. The first customer doesn't have a middle name and second has one. Both are valid. However, the first customer name will be invalid if you remove the question mark from the middle_name in the name declaration in the DTD because the first customer doesn't have a middle name.

```
<name>
   <first_name>Bob</first_name>
   <last_name>Smith</last_name>
</name>
<name>
   <first_name>Bob</first_name>
   <middle_name>Alex</middle_name>
   <last_name>Smith</last_name>
</name>
```

We show you a good example of zero to many in our original XML example. The customers tag may contain zero to many customer elements. You may have a process where you transmit a file every day, whether or not there are any new records. There are many business cases where you'll need a positive confirmation that there haven't been any new customers that day.

Now you can change the business rule a little bit and say that you only want the file transmitted if at least one customer is defined. If this is the business rule, then you can change the definition of the customers element so it has one to many customer elements.

Optional Child Elements

The declaration of a parent element contains the names of child elements that are contained within the parent, which we discussed earlier in this chapter. However, all those child elements must be present for the XML document to be valid. If one is missing, then the entire document is invalid.

There is a way to make child elements optional: You use the OR (|) operator when specifying child elements in the parent's declaration. We illustrate this in the next example, which uses the OR operator to make phone numbers optional:

```
<!ELEMENT phone (business|cell|home)>
```

This example declares the phone element as a parent that could contain either a business phone number, cellular phone number, or a home phone number, but not more than one. If you write the declaration like this, then the XML document must contains all three telephone numbers. Leaving out one of them invalidates the document.

```
<!ELEMENT phone (business, cell, home)>
```

However, by separating the names of the child element with the OR operator, the parser is told that the XML document is still valid if one—and only one—of those phone numbers is in the document.

This means the following portion of the XML document is valid because it contains one phone number:

```
<phone>
   <cell>555-555-5432</cell>
</phone>
```

However, this portion is invalid because it contains multiple telephone numbers.

```
<phone>
   <business>555-555-1212</business>
   <cell>555-555-5432</cell>
</phone>
```

Grouping Elements

Here's a common problem: A company may have more than one address, each with its own telephone number. How do you declare this within a DTD? This is tricky because the solution isn't obvious. The answer is to group the address and phone child elements and use the + symbol (see Table 3-1) to specify that the group can appear multiple times within the XML document.

You group child elements by placing them within parentheses as we show in the next example. You'll notice that the address and phone child elements form a group. Any symbol that follows the parenthesis affects all members of the group. So in this case, the + symbol tells the parser that there can be one to many occurrences of the address and phone child elements within each customer tag.

```
<!ELEMENT customer (name, title, company,
        (address, phone)+, email, account_number)>
```

If you replace the customer declaration in the DTD we show at the beginning of this chapter with this one, then the following XML document is valid, even though the customer contains more than one address and phone number. This is because the address and phone child elements form a group that could have many occurrences within the customer tag.

```
<!DOCTYPE customers SYSTEM "customers.dtd">
<customers>
   <customer>
      <name>
        <first_name>Bob</first_name>
        <last_name>Smith</last_name>
      </name>
      <title>Manager</title>
      <company>My Company Inc.</company>
      <address>
         <street_1>The Tech Building</street_1>
         <street_2>555 5th Street</street_2>
         <city>Some City</city>
         <state>NJ</state>
         <zip>07665</zip>
      </address>
      <phone>
         <business>555-555-1212</business>
         <cell>555-555-5432</cell>
         <home>555-555-7678</home>
         <fax>555-555-9989</fax>
      </phone>
      <address>
         <street_1>The Other Tech Building</street_1>
         <street_2>124 Main Street</street_2>
         <city>Some Other City</city>
         <state>NY</state>
         <zip>10001</zip>
      </address>
      <phone>
         <business>555-312-1212</business>
         <cell>555-324-5432</cell>
         <home>555-556-7678</home>
         <fax>555-768-9989</fax>
      </phone>
      <email>bsmith@mycompany.com</email>
      <account_number>6970654</account_number>
   </customer>
</customers>
```

EMPTY and ANY Elements

Two other useful element declarations are EMPTY and ANY. An EMPTY element indicates that the element does not have a child node. That is, it doesn't have child elements or PCDATA. An ANY element means that anything can be used as a child element.

The image element (img) is a good example of an EMPTY element because an image element doesn't contain data. It does reference an image file, but the reference is an attribute of the element rather than information contained within the element. Here's how an EMPTY element is declared:

```
<!ELEMENT img EMPTY>
```

Here's how the EMPTY element is used within an XML document:

```
<img src="image.gif">
```

You commonly use the ANY element when you're updating a DTD to accommodate multiple versions of XML. If you're changing the definition of the XML, ANY gives you a way to loosely define the XML. Suppose the address isn't part of the original DTD. Now you want to make it required but it's going to take some time for all the partners to update their processes. You can have the customer tag contain ANY elements during this transition. The use of ANY is very strongly discouraged because it doesn't provide a concise definition of the document. It was only added to the specification to be used when there's no other practical way to deal with updating and redefining documents.

Naming Elements

You have great flexibility when naming elements in your DTD so long as your names conform to the rules. Here are those rules:

- Begin element names with a letter, colon, or underscore followed by a combination of letters, numbers, underscores, periods, colons, or hyphens.
- White space is not permitted within the name.
- Avoid using a colon in the name so the element isn't confused with namespaces, which uses a colon in its name.
- Avoid starting the element name with XML because this is reserved for XML standards.
- Keep element names short and concise. Although there isn't any limit placed on the length of the name, some XML processors may restrict the length of element names.

Attribute Declarations

An *attribute declaration* defines an attribute for an element. An *attribute* is information that describes an aspect of the element. For example, customer ID and customer type might be attributes for a customer element.

Attributes are declared in an attribute list within the document type definition. The attribute list contains the name of the element and a declaration of each attribute. Here's how to declare attributes for the customer element:

```
<!ATTLIST customer
   cust_id (CDATA) #REQUIRED
   type (retail|wholesale) "retail">
```

You use the ATTLIST keyword to identify the declaration of the attribute list. Next to ATTLIST is the name of the element, which is customer in this example. Each subsequent line declares an attribute.

The first attribute is called cust_id and is declared as character data (CDATA). The #REQUIRED keyword indicates that this attribute must be present for every customer. (It doesn't need a value—cust_id="" would be perfectly valid XML because the attribute is present.) That is, an error message is generated if there is a customer element that doesn't contain a cust_id attribute. Table 3-2 lists other keywords that are used to describe the form of an attribute.

The last line in the code declares type as an attribute. Valid values for this attribute are contained within the parentheses. These are retail or wholesale. The pipe (|) is the OR operator. Only one of these values is considered a valid option. Any other values cause an error message to generate when the XML document is processed. Notice that retail is repeated within quotations. This is the default value for this attribute. If no type is entered, then the parser uses retail as the value for the type attribute.

Here's how these attributes are used in an XML document:

```
<customer cust_id="55323" type="retail">
   ...
</customer>
```

Form	Description
#REQUIRED	The attribute is required but doesn't have any specific default value.
#FIXED	The attribute is only allowed to have one value. The attribute itself may be optional, but if it is present in the XML document, it can only have this value.
#IMPLIED	The value is not required and no default value is provided.
"VALUE"	The text contained within the quotes is the default value.

Table 3-2 Forms of Attribute Values

This, too, is valid, although the type attribute isn't assigned a value in the XML document. Remember that the type attribute is declared with a default value. Therefore, the parser automatically assigns the default value, which is retail, to the type attribute when the type attribute is assigned a value in the XML document.

```
<customer cust_id="55323">
   ...
</customer>
```

Entity Declarations

An entity may refer to a block of text, an external file, an alias name, or other forms of referencing. The parser processes some entities. These are referred to as *parsed entities.* Other entities are not parsed and are called *unparsed entities.*

Parsed and unparsed entities are identified by the absence or presence of a special character in the entity declaration. If the entity contains <, ?, &, ', ", or #, then characters following the special character and up to the next whitespace character (i.e., space) are not parsed. All other characters are parsed.

You can create your own unparsed characters within the document type definition. Here's how you do it. Suppose you want to use NJ as an alias name for New Jersey so that you can use &NJ wherever you want New Jersey to appear in an XML document and have the parser replace &NJ with New Jersey during processing.

First you need to declare NJ as an unparsed element in the DTD using the following code:

```
<!ENTITY NJ "New Jersey">
```

Then you can use this code in your XML document whenever you want to use New Jersey:

```
<state>&NJ;</state>
```

The parser replaces &NJ; with New Jersey during processing just as if the XML document contains this:

```
<state>New Jersey</state>
```

Looking Ahead

You use the document type definition (DTD) to declare tags that can be used in an XML document. There are two types of DTDs, those internal to the XML document and those that are external, which are contained in a separate file. You can reference an external DTD among many XML documents by using the SYSTEM keyword followed by the name of the external DTD file.

An external DTD can be divided into subsets called shared DTD. A subset declares some elements. Subsets are then referenced with the DTD, which inherits the element declared in the subset.

You can modify elements declared in a DTD by using symbols to indicate the number of occurrences of a child element within a parent element. This enables an element to be repeated multiple times in an XML document or not be included from the XML document. You can group child elements within the declaration of the parent element, enabling you to treat the group of elements as one.

Attributes are data related to an element such as a customer type. You declare attributes in an attribute list by using the keyword ATTLIST. The attribute list can specify valid values for an attribute as well as a default value.

An entity is a form of reference such as an alias name. Some entities are parsed and others are unparsed. Unparsed entities begin with a special character, which the parser ignores.

Quiz

1. An XML document must contain all elements declared in the DTD.
   a. True
   b. False
2. #PCDATA refers to
   a. Parsed charter data
   b. Program character data
   c. Parsed character data
   d. None of the above
3. A question mark following the name of a child name in the declaration of a parent element means
   a. The child element is required.
   b. The child element is optional.
   c. The name of the child element is unknown.
   d. One occurrence of the child element is required.

4. What is address, phone in the declaration <!ELEMENT customer (company, (address, phone)+, email)> ?
   a. A group
   b. The value of address and phone is concatenated.
   c. The value of email is concatenated to the value of address and phone.
   d. The value of email is concatenated to the value of phone.
5. What is this: <!ENTITY % phone SYSTEM “phone.dtd”>?
   a. A reference to the internal DTD called phone.dtd
   b. A reference to the phone system
   c. References a shared DTD
   d. References the phone.dtd XML document
6. An image tag is an example of an EMPTY element.
   a. True
   b. False
7. All XML markup tags must have an attribute.
   a. True
   b. False
8. An element name can begin with
   a. A colon
   b. An underscore
   c. Letters
   d. All of the above
9. You cannot set valid options when declaring an attribute.
   a. True
   b. False
10. #REQUIRED specifies that an element is required in all XML documents that use the DTD.
    a. True
    b. False

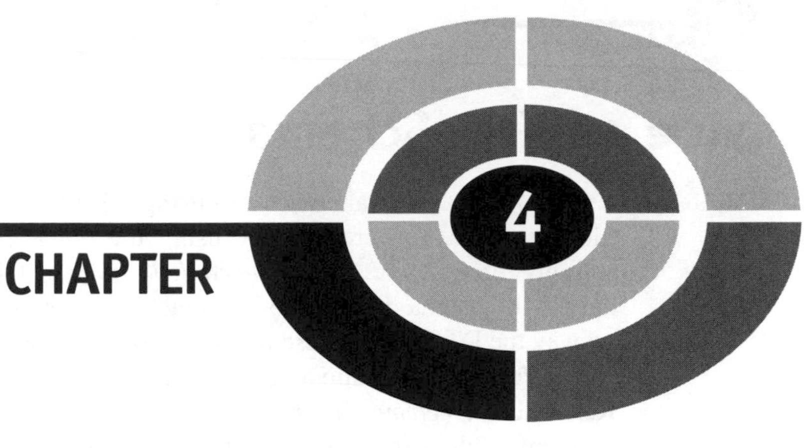

CHAPTER 4

XML Schema

As we discussed in Chapter 3, a parser is software you use to extract data from an XML document. However, before it does this, the parser must learn about the XML tags used to describe data in the document.

The parser has no way of knowing the XML tags unless you tell it what they are by creating a document type definition (DTD), which you learned how to do in Chapter 3. A DTD describes the structure of the XML document by defining XML tags used in the document and relationships among these tags.

However, there is another way you can describe the structure of an XML document: You can create an *XML schema*. An XML schema does everything a DTD does and more, which is why many developers have switched to using it. In this chapter, you'll learn how to take advantage of an XML schema in your application.

Inside an XML Schema

An XML schema is an alternative to using a DTD to describe the structure of an XML document. You create it by using the XML schema language, which is commonly referred to as *XML schema definition* (XSD).

An XML schema defines the building blocks of an XML document much the same way the DTD does. These building blocks consist of elements, attributes, and the parent/child relationship among elements.

Remember, an *element* is an XML tag, and an *attribute* is information related to an element, such as an account number for the XML tag customer. A child element contains data. A parent element contains other parent elements and child elements. Recall that the customer element that you defined in Chapter 3 was a parent element and contained child elements such as the customer cell phone number. It also contained the customer name element, which is itself a parent element because it contains customer first name and customer last name tags as shown here:

```
<customer>
   <name>
      <firstname />
      <lastname />
   </name>
</customer>
```

You can define the same structure in an XML schema. However, an XML schema has the capability of defining more than the descriptions found in a DTD. In an XML schema you can also define data types and namespaces.

You define a data type to eliminate any confusion that might arise with interpreting the data the XML tag describes. For example, many XML documents contain dates such as March 6, 2007. However, the format of the date can vary depending on your country. Here are common ways a date is represented in an XML document:

3/6/2007
03-06-2007
3-6-2007
6-3-2007
2007 March 6
March 6, 2007
6 March 2007

All of these are valid dates. However, the parser might become confused unless you specifically define the data type of the date. The data type tells the parser the format used to represent a date in the XML document.

Here's how the data type is defined in an XML schema. This defines the data type "date" as year-month-day. The parser considers other date formats errors if it encounters them when processing the XML document. There are also predefined formats for time as well as date/time, which you'll learn about later in this chapter.

```
<date type="date">2007-03-06</date>
```

Likewise, you can define an integer data type in this way. You can define positive and negative integers. If you omit the sign, then + is assumed.

```
<id type="integer">87326</id>
```

Document Type Definition vs. XML Schema

Let's take a closer look at an XML schema by starting with an XML document. Here's an XML document that defines customers. The customers element contains a customer child element. This customer element contains two child elements: firstname and lastname. Of course, a real XML document would contain more data about a customer, but we'll keep the document brief for illustration purposes.

```
<?xml  version="1.0"?>
<customers>
  <customer>
    <firstname>Mary</firstname>
    <lastname>Smith</lastname>
  </customer>
</customers>
```

You need to define the customers, customer, firstname, and lastname XML tags in order for the parser to process this document. We'll define these first using a DTD and then using an XML schema so you can compare both techniques.

Here's the DTD that describes the structure of the previous XML document. Notice there are two parent tags and two data elements. The first parent tag is customers, which contains the customer tag. The customer tag is also a parent tag and contains the firstname and lastname tags. The firstname and lastname tags are data elements that contain information about the customer. Save this DTD into the customers.dtd file.

```
<!ELEMENT customers (customer*)>
<!ELEMENT customer (firstname, lastname)>
<!ELEMENT firstname (#PCDATA)>
<!ELEMENT lastname (#PCDATA)>
```

Next you must reference the DTD file in the XML document. You do this with the <!DOCTYPE> tag, as you'll recall from Chapter 3. We illustrate this in the update of the XML document that follows. The parser reads the customers.dtd file when it encounters the <!DOCTYPE> tag in the XML document to learn about the tags before processing the XML document.

```
<?xml  version="1.0"?>
<!DOCTYPE customers SYSTEM "customers.dtd">
<customers>
  <customer>
    <firstname>Mary</firstname>
    <lastname>Smith</lastname>
  </customer>
</customers>
```

Now let's take a look at how you use the XML schema in place of the DTD. You use the XML schema language to create the XML schema. Each statement of an XLM schema begins with <xs: and is followed by the keyword in the XML schema language.

You'll learn the XML schema language throughout this chapter; however, first, we'll show you an XML schema that's equivalent to the customers.dtd DTD. Here's the XML schema. At first glance, you'll probably notice there are few similarities between a DTD and an XML schema, although both define the structure of an XML document.

```
<?xml version="1.0"?>
<xs:schema xmlns:xs="http://www.w3.org/2001/XMLSchema">
<xs:element name="customers">
  <xs:element name="customer">
    <xs:complexType>
      <xs:sequence>
        <xs:element name="firstname" type="xs:string"/>
        <xs:element name="lastname" type="xs:string"/>
      </xs:sequence>
    </xs:complexType>
  <.xs:element>
</xs:element>
</xs:schema>
```

The XML schema begins with the xs:schema tag. This tag contains the xmlns:xs attribute that points to the XMLSchema specifications used to write the XML schema. (You'll find these specifications on the www.w3.org web site.)

The XML schema then proceeds to define the customers element and the customer element, which are similar to those in the DTD. The customer tag is defined as having a complexType, which is a DTD and a particular sequence of elements.

The customer element is a parent element that contains firstname and lastname elements, which is also similar to the one in the DTD. However, notice that these elements are defined as a string data type. This is unique to the XML schema. We'll examine each component of an XML schema in detail in "An Inside Look at an XML Schema."

You save the XML schema to a file called customers.xsd. Next you'll need to reference the customers.xsd file from within the XML document. You do this by inserting the xsi:schemaLocation attribute into the customers tag within the XML document. We illustrate this in the next revision of the XML document. When the parser encounters the xsi:schemaLocation attribute, it reads the customers.xsd XML schema and then applies it to the XML document.

```
<?xml version="1.0"?>
<customers xmlns:xsi="http://www.w3.org/2001/XMLSchema-in-
stance"
xsi:schemaLocation="customers.xsd">

  <customer>
    <firstname>Mary</firstname>
    <lastname>Smith</lastname>
  </customer>
</customers>
```

An Inside Look at an XML Schema

An XML schema begins with the xs:schema tag, which is the outermost tag and encloses all the elements of the XML schema. Typically the xs:schema tag includes attributes, especially the xmlns:xs="http://www.w3.org/2001/XMLSchema" attribute. This attribute specifies that elements and data types contained in the XML schema are defined in the 2001 XMLSchema namespace (found at www.w3.org/2001/XMLSchema).

The xmlns:xs is the name of the attribute and states that elements and data types for the XML schema should have the xs prefix. You can use any prefix within the XML schema to define elements and data types, but the xs prefix is preferred.

Here's the basic structure of an XML schema:

```
<?xml version="1.0"?>
<xs:schema xmlns:xs="http://www.w3.org/2001/XMLSchema">
 ......
</xs:schema>
```

You reference an XML schema from within an XML document by referring to an instance of the XML schema using the following two attributes in the first tag in the XML document:

```
xmlns:xsi="http://www.w3.org/2001/XMLSchema-instance"
       xsi:schemaLocation="customers.xsd"
```

The xmlns:xsi attribute declares an instance of the XML schema, which is defined in XMLSchema-instance located at www.w3.org/2001/XMLSchema-instance. This gives you the location of the DTD. XMLSchema is built on top of a DTD.

The xsi:schemaLocation attribute identifies the file that contains the XML schema that will be used when parsing the XML document. You can store the XML schema using any file name; however, the name should imply the nature of the XML schema and end with the xsd file extension. The location can be a URL.

Defining Simple Elements

You define elements of the XML schema within the <xs:schema>...</xs:schema> tags. The most common of these is the *simple element*. A simple element contains text and has no child elements and no attributes. However, the text can be defined using a data type such as date, integer, float, or one of the other data types mentioned in the next paragraph.

For example, a simple element is defined:

```
<xs:element name="ElementName" type="ElementType"/>
```

The *name attribute* defines the name of the element and the type attribute defines the element's data type. Here are the data types that are most often used in an XML schema:

```
xs:string
xs:boolean
xs:decimal
xs:float
xs:double
xs:dateTime
xs:time
xs:date
```

For many XML schemas, you'll want to define a *default value* for an element. The parser automatically uses the default value if the XML document doesn't provide a value for the element. A default value is defined as an attribute of the element.

Let's say that you're defining a simple element called format. Data within the format tag specifies the format of the document. The format will be in the xs:string data types. The default value is Portable Document Format (PDF), which is a format used by Adobe Acrobat Reader. Here's an element that defines the value as "PDF":

```
<format>PDF</format>
```

If you want the default to be PDF, this is how you would define it in the XML schema:

```
<xs:element name="format" type="xs:string" default="PDF"/>
```

Sometimes the value associated with an element must be a specified value. That is, when you create the XML document using the XML schema, you must insert a specific value into the tag. You can specify the value that must be inserted into the tag by inserting the fixed attribute into your tag.

The *fixed attribute* defines the value for the tag. If you don't place the value in the tag, the parser automatically uses the value that's associated with the fixed attribute.

Here's how to define the fixed attribute:

```
<xs:element name="format" type="xs:string" fixed="PDF"/>
```

Defining Attributes

An *attribute* is information about an element. Let's say that the element is called car and an attribute of the car element is color, which is the color of the car. The value of the color attribute is the actual color.

An attribute is defined in the XML schema using the xs:attribute tag. The xs: attribute tag itself requires two attributes: name and type. The *name attribute* is the name of the attribute you're defining. The *type attribute* is the data type of the attribute you're defining.

Here's how to define the attribute color. The name of the attribute is color and it's a string data type. This means that any value assigned to the color attribute in the XML document will be treated as a string, even if an integer is used as its value.

```
<xs:attribute name="color" type="xs:string"/>
```

You can specify a default value by using the default attribute in the attribute definition. The default attribute requires you to supply the default value for the attribute that you're defining. This value is used if the attribute is excluded from the corresponding element in the XML document.

Here's how to set the default value. Green is used as the color any time this attribute is excluded from the XML document.

```
<xs:attribute name="color" type="xs:string"
default="green"/>
```

There might come a time when you want to set the value for the attribute, such as if you were writing an XML schema for Henry Ford, who offered customers any color Model T Ford as long as it was black.

You set the value of an attribute in the XML schema by using the fixed attribute. The value of the fixed attribute becomes the value of the attribute in the XML document. Here's how you use the fixed attribute. An error occurs if you attempt to assign a value other than the fixed value to the attribute.

```
<xs:attribute name="color" type="xs:string" fixed="black"/>
```

You can define an attribute as being required or optional depending on the nature of your XML document. You do this by using the use attribute in the attribute's definition. The use attribute accepts one of two values: required or optional. As the name implies, a *required value* mandates that a value be assigned to the attribute within the XML document. Failure to do this generates an error. An *optional value* doesn't require that a value be set for the attribute.

Here's how to specify whether or not the attribute is required. Of course, you would use only one of these statements in your XML schema since an attribute can be either required or optional, but not both.

```
<xs:attribute name="color" type="xs:string" use="required"/>
<xs:attribute name="color" type="xs:string" use="optional"/>
```

You can use an attribute in an XML document once it's defined in the XML schema that's associated with the XML document. Here's how the color attribute would appear within the car element of an XML document:

```
<car color="red">
   ...
</car>
```

Facets

A *facet* is a valid value that can be assigned to an attribute. Suppose the car manufacturer offers a car in black, blue, red, or green, but not in any other color. Each of these colors is a valid value that can be assigned to the color attribute.

You can restrict an attribute's value to a set of valid values by using the xs: restriction tag within the definition of the attribute. The restriction tag lists valid values. Values that aren't listed generate an error if you assign them to the attribute within the XML document.

The xs:restriction tag is a parent tag that contains one or more xs:enumeration tags, each one specifying a valid value for the attribute. The xs:enumeration tag has one attribute called value that's assigned the valid value. You can have as many xs: enumeration tags as is necessary for your XML document.

Let's enhance the definition of the color attribute to limit the color choices to black, blue, red, and green. Here's the revised definition:

```
<xs:attribute name="color" type="colorType"/>
<xs:simpleType name="colorType">
  <xs:restriction base="xs:string">
    <xs:enumeration value="black"/>
    <xs:enumeration value="blue"/>
    <xs:enumeration value="red"/>
    <xs:enumeration value="green"/>
  </xs:restriction>
</xs:simpleType>
```

You'll notice that we modified this definition. The first change occurs in the type attribute. We changed the type from xs:string to colorType. The colorType is a data type that's defined on the second line as a xs:simpleType.

The definition xs:simpleType contains the xs:restriction tag and related xs: enumeration tag. Here's what we're saying: ColorType is an xs:simpleType that's restricted to four xs:strings that are itemized as the value of the xs:enumeration tags. Any time an attribute is defined as a colorType data type, that attribute can only be assigned black, blue, red, or green as its value; otherwise an error is generated.

For example, the following is valid:

```
<car color="black">
```

And the following is invalid:

```
<car color="yellow">
```

Ranges

Sometimes you'll need to specify a range of numbers as valid values for an element, such as a range of valid temperatures. You can do this by using the xs:minInclusive and xs:maxInclusive tags within the restriction tag of the xs:element definition.

Let's say that that valid range is from 32 through 212. Here's how you incorporate this into a definition of an element within an XML schema. You'll notice that this definition resembles the previous definition of an attribute. Both define a xs:

simpleType, although they are given two different names—and two different definitions. The value of the temperature element must be an xs:decimal value between 32 and 212 inclusive. Any value outside this range causes an error.

```
<xs:element name="temperature" type="temperatureType"/>
<xs:simpleType name="temperatureType">
  <xs:restriction base="xs:decimal">
    <xs:minInclusive value="32"/>
    <xs:maxInclusive value="212"/>
  </xs:restriction>
</xs:simpleType>
```

With this definition, the following value in an XML document is valid:

```
<temperature>120</temperature>
```

And this value is invalid and causes an error.

```
<temperature>350</temperature>
```

You can also use maxExclusive and minExclusive. Exclusive doesn't include the boundary value. That is, Exclusive is equivalent to "greater than," and Exclusive is equivalent to "greater than or equal to."

Regular Expressions

You can enforce stricter restrictions on values that can be used as elements in an XML document by incorporating a regular expression in the definition of an element. A *regular expression* is a pattern of characters that defines the kinds, and format, of characters that can be entered into an element of an XML document.

Unfortunately, showing you how to create regular expressions is beyond the scope of this book. However, you can learn about regular expressions by reading *C++: The Complete Reference, Fourth Edition* by Herb Schildt (McGraw-Hill/Osborne, 2002).

Once you learn how to create a regular expression, you can use it in the definition of an element to restrict the contents of the element. Here's how you do this. Let's say that you define an element that contains a zip code. A zip code contains five digits. Each digit can be from zero through nine. This is written as a regular expression as [0-9] {5}. This reads: a digit from zero through nine, five digits.

A regular expression is assigned as the value to the value attribute of the xs: pattern tag in the XML schema, as shown in this definition of the 5_digit_zip element. You'll notice that this element is defined in a way similar to the element in the previous section of this chapter was defined; however, the xs:pattern tag is used to restrict the contents of the element.

```
<xs:element name="5_digit_zip">
  <xs:simpleType>
    <xs:restriction base="xs:string">
      <xs:pattern value="[0-9]{5}"/>
    </xs:restriction>
  </xs:simpleType>
</xs:element>
```

Another common use for a regular expression is to limit the content of an element to only lowercase characters. You do this by using ([a–z]) * as the regular expression. This is read as zero or more occurrences of characters that fall into the range a–z.

Here's how this regular expression looks in the definition of the lowercase element:

```
<xs:element name="lowercase">
  <xs:simpleType>
    <xs:restriction base="xs:string">
      <xs:pattern value="([a-z])*"/>
    </xs:restriction>
  </xs:simpleType>
</xs:element>
```

If you want only uppercase letters entered, then you use ([A–Z]) *. And you use ([a–zA–Z])* if you want to restrict the contents to lowercase and uppercase letters only.

You can use a regular expression to specify valid values for an attribute, too. You accomplish this by using the OR (|) regular expression operator. The OR operator separates alternative valid values that can be used for an attribute.

Let's return to the color attribute for the car element. Here's the way you could specify that the color can be black, blue, red or green.

```
<xs:attribute name="color"/>
<xs:simpleType>
  <xs:restriction base="xs:string">
    <xs:pattern value="black|blue|red|green"/>
  </xs:restriction>
</xs:simpleType>
</xs:attribute>
```

Working with Whitespace Characters

Each character on your keyboard is assigned a unique number called an *ASCII number*. You don't need to know these numbers, but if you're curious, look up "ASCII table" in a search engine and you'll see the ASCII numbers.

Some characters are nonprintable characters, such as a space inserted when you press the spacebar or the tab when you press the TAB key. These are referred to as whitespace characters. You'll find a list of these characters numbered from zero to 33 on the ASCII table.

Whitespace characters are inserted into a document to give instructions to the program that reads the document. You don't see these on the screen, but a program, such as a parser, can see them.

For example, a carriage return and linefeed whitespace characters are inserted into a document when you press the ENTER key. This gives the program instructions to move the cursor to the beginning of the next line.

You can tell the parser how to handle whitespace characters that appear in an XML document by using the xs:whiteSpace tag in the XML schema. There are three things that you can do when you encounter a whitespace character in an XML document: preserve, replace, or collapse.

Preserve means that the parser does nothing special with the whitespace character. It simply passes the whitespace characters along with the rest of the XML document. *Replace* tells the parse to replace all whitespace characters with a space. *Collapse* tells the parser to replace all whitespace characters with spaces (similar to replace), then it collapses multiple occurrences of whitespaces to a single space. Furthermore, leading and trailing whitespaces are deleted.

You specify preserve, replace, and collapse as the value of the value attribute of the xs:whiteSpace tag. Here is an example of preserve:

```
<xs:element name="description">
  <xs:simpleType>
    <xs:restriction base="xs:string">
      <xs:whiteSpace value="preserve"/>
    </xs:restriction>
  </xs:simpleType>
</xs:element>
```

Restricting the Length of a Field

A seemingly endless number of characters can be used as the content of an element. However, other applications that use the data might restrict the number of characters they can receive from the XML document.

Let's say that the lastname element of an XML document contains a name that is 40 characters long. After the parser processes the XML document, the lastname is sent to a column of a table in a database. The column permits up 35 characters. This means five characters are truncated.

A common solution to this problem is to limit the number of characters that can be contained in the element. You can do this by using the xs:maxLength tag in the XML schema. The xs:maxLength has a value attribute that's assigned the maximum number of characters that can be placed in the element. An error occurs if the content exceeds this value.

Here's how to set the maximum value of an element. This sets the maximum length to 30 characters:

```
<xs:element name="firstname">
  <xs:simpleType>
    <xs:restriction base="xs:string">
      <xs:maxLength value="30"/>
    </xs:restriction>
  </xs:simpleType>
</xs:element>
```

Besides setting the maximum length, you can also set a minimum length for an element or fix its length to a specific number of characters. You set the minimum length by using the xs:minLength tag, and set the fixed length by using the xs:length tag. Both of these are illustrated here. Each is placed within the xs:restriction tag.

```
<xs:minLength value="1"/>
<xs:length value="20"/>
```

Complex Elements

A *complex element* is an XML element that contains other elements and may contain attributes. Think of a complex element as a subset of an XML document, such as the customer element we show here. The customer element contains the firstname, middlename, and lastname elements to form a complex element:

```
<customer>
   <firstname>Mary</firstname>
   <middlename>Ellen</middlename>
   <lastname>Smith</lastname>
</customer>
```

There are several ways you can define a complex element in an XML schema. One way is to define a complex type when defining the element. We illustrate this in the next example, which defines the customer element. You use the xs:complexType tag to define the other elements that comprise the complex element. Notice that we've used the xs:sequence tag here. This specifies that the other elements must appear in the XML document in the same sequence they appear in this definition.

```
<xs:element name="customer">
  <xs:complexType>
    <xs:sequence>
      <xs:element name="firstname" type="xs:string"/>
      <xs:element name="middlename" type="xs:string"/>
      <xs:element name="lastname" type="xs:string"/>
    </xs:sequence>
  </xs:complexType>
</xs:element>
```

An error occurs if they appear out of sequence. For example, this generates an error with the preceding schema because the middlename is before the firstname. They must appear in the order specified.

```
<customer>
   <middlename>Ellen</middlename>
   <firstname>Mary</firstname>
   <lastname>Smith</lastname>
</customer>
```

Previously in this chapter you learned that you could create a parent-child relationship between elements. This is the case with the customer element. The customer element is the parent and the complexType—not the individual elements—is the child. Therefore, the customer element has one child: the complexType.

There is a drawback to defining a complexType within the definition of an element. You cannot use the complexType outside of the element. That is, you can't use firstname, middlename, and lastname without using customer.

At first glance this may not seem important because a customer has a first name, middle name, and last name. However, consider other kinds of people referenced in an XML document, such as employees, vendors, and others who have a first name, middle name, and last name. You would have to repeat the definition of this complexType for each kind of person who's described in an XML document.

A more efficient technique is to define a complexType outside of the element and give it a unique name. You then use the name of the complexType any time you want to refer to elements defined in the complexType.

Let's redefine the nameinfo complexType as a stand-alone type. This is practically the same definition except you've given the complexType a name—nameinfo.

```
  <xs:complexType name="nameinfo">
    <xs:sequence>
      <xs:element name="firstname" type="xs:string"/>
      <xs:element name="middlename" type="xs:string"/>
      <xs:element name="lastname" type="xs:string"/>
    </xs:sequence>
  </xs:complexType>
```

Now you can define an element as being a nameinfo type. When doing this, the new element inherits the firstname, middlename, and lastname elements just as if it were defined within the definition of the element.

Here's how to designate an element as a nameinfo type. You'll notice that we've included the definition of the complexType in this example:

```
<xs:element name="customer" type="nameinfo"/>
<xs:element name="salesperson" type="nameinfo"/>
<xs:element name="manager" type="nameinfo"/>
<xs:complexType name="nameinfo">
   <xs:sequence>
      <xs:element name="firstname" type="xs:string"/>
      <xs:element name="middlename" type="xs:string"/>
      <xs:element name="lastname" type="xs:string"/>
   </xs:sequence>
</xs:complexType>
```

Setting the Number of Occurrences

In Chapter 3, you learned how to specify the number of times an element and its children can be used in an XML document using a DTD. You can do something similar in an XML schema by using the minOccurs and maxOccurs attributes.

The value of the minOccurs attribute determines the minimum number of times that an element must appear in the XML document. The value of the maxOccurs attribute determines the maximum number of occurrences for an element. You include the minOccurs and maxOccurs when you define the element, as shown here:

```
<xs:element name="customer" minOccurs="0"maxOccurs="unbounded">
```

In this example, the customer element can appear zero times—that is, it doesn't have to be used in the XML document—and unbounded. *Unbounded* means an unlimited number of times. Table 4-1 shows a comparison between defining the number of occurrences using the DTD and using minOccurs and maxOccurs in the XML schema.

Number of Occurrences	DTD	minOccurs	maxOccurs
Zero to many	*	Zero	Unbounded
One to many	+	One	Unbounded
Zero or one	?	Zero	One

Table 4-1 A Comparison Between minOccurs and maxOccurs

If you don't specify the minOccurs and maxOccurs attributes, the default value is one.

With DTDs you learned how to reference multiple DTDs to form the definition of an XML document. An XML schema has a similar mechanism. You can use xs: include, which is basically the same as copying and pasting the referenced schema into the current schema. It doesn't allow for any type of override of or alteration to the schema. The syntax looks like this:

```
<xs:include schemaLocation="customer.xsd"/>
```

This tells the processor to include the customer.xsd definition. You can also use xs:redefine to include an external schema. xs:redefine allows you to alter the definitions in the remote file:

```
<xs:redefine schemaLocation="customer.xsd"/>
   … new definitions …
</xs:redefine>
```

Looking Ahead

An XML schema is another way to describe the structure of an XML document. The XML schema defines the building blocks used to build the XML document, similar in concept to the document type definition (DTD).

The XML schema language is used to create the XML schema. Each statement in the XML schema languge begins with <xs: and is followed by a keyword. The first statement contains the xs:schema tag that identifies it as an XML schema.

An element is defined by using the xs:element tag that contains a name attribute, which identifies the name of the element and a type attribute that identifies the data type of the element. The data type can be one of the predefined data types or a data type that you defined, such as a complexType.

You define your own attributes for an element by using the xs:attribute tag. This tag also requires that you specify a name of the attribute, which is assigned to the name attribute, and a type attribute, which is the data type of the attribute. Optionally, you can define a default value, define a fixed value, and indicate whether the attribute is required or optional.

A facet is a valid value that can be assigned to an attribute. You define facets by using the xs:restriction and xs:enumeration tags. The xs:restriction tag states there are restrictions imposed on the attribute, and the xs:enumeration tag specifies those restrictions. You can set restrictions in the form of a range of values or specify more complex restrictions by using a regular expression.

You can create your own data type as either simpleType or complexType. You use a simpleType when defining one element, and a complexType when defining multiple elements.

Quiz

1. An XML schema is used to define a complex type.
   a. True
   b. False
2. type="integer" means
   a. The content of an element is the word integer.
   b. All types except integers can be used in the corresponding element.
   c. Only integers can be used in the corresponding element.
   d. None of the above.
3. xmlns:xs="http://www.w3.org/2001/XMLSchema" is used to
   a. Identify ownership of the XML schema
   b. Identify ownership of the XML document
   c. Identify the XML schema specifications used in the XML schema
   d. Identify that this is an XML schema
4. The xs:sequence tag
   a. Specifies the sequence in which elements must appear in an XML document
   b. Specifies the sequence in which elements must appear in an XML schema

c. Specifies the sequence in which attributes must appear in an XML document

d. Specifies the sequence in which attributes must appear in an XML schema

5. xsi:schemaLocation="customers.xsd" is used to

a. Identify the owner of the XML document

b. Identify the owner of the XML schema

c. Identify the location of the XML document

d. Identify the location of the XML schema

6. You can require a specific value for an attribute by setting the value for fixed.

a. True

b. False

7. A regular expression can be used to specify complex restrictions for the content of an element.

a. True

b. False

8. You can specify a series of valid values for an element by using which of the following in a regular expression?

a. |

b. OR

c. or

d. +

9. A facet is a valid value that can be assigned to an attribute.

a. True

b. False

10. The xs:enumeration tag is used to define a valid value for an attribute.

a. True

b. False

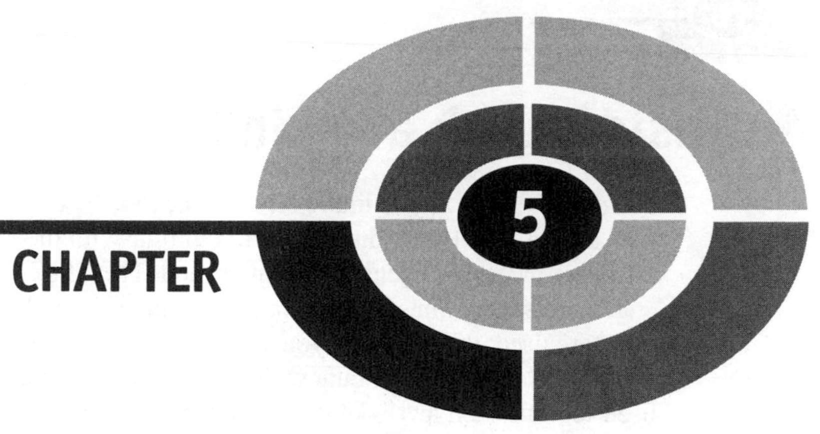

XLink, XPath, XPointer

Real-world XML documents can become complex and difficult to navigate, especially if they reference multiple external resources, such as other documents and images. Professional XML developers use XML's version of a global position satellite to find elements within the XML document.

XML's global position satellite system has nothing to do with satellites. It simply provides three clever features that you can use to find your way around the document. These features are *XLink, XPath,* and *XPointer.*

XLink hooks up your document with any number of external resources while XPath and XPointer show your parser how to navigate around the document to find the piece of the document that you need to process.

Sounds confusing? We'll, it won't be by the time you finish this chapter.

An Inside Look at XLink

XLink is XML's way of linking a resource to a specific behavior. This might sound new to you, but it shouldn't if you're familiar with the way HTML links resources. XLink is basically a generalization of the HTML link.

Before seeing how XLink works, let's take a step back and review how HTML links are used; this will give you a foundation for understanding how to use XLink. An HTML link is an attribute within an anchor tag, such as the href attribute, that's used to define a hyperlink, as we show here. The anchor tag can link to a resource such as this HTML page or to a location within the same page, which is called a *relative link.*

```
<a href="some_page.html">
```

Another common link is used in the img tag to link the src attribute to an image file, as we show here. The image file is an external resource to the web page and gets pulled into the current document. The browser loads the HTML page, parses it, and finds the image tag, then makes the request to the server for this resource.

```
<img src="image.gif">
```

Tags that are associated with links exhibit a certain behavior based on a given link's attribute. For example, the href attribute enables the anchor tag to jump to another page or to a different location on the same page. If the target attribute is used within the anchor tag, then the other page is displayed in a new browser window, as we show here.

```
<a href="some_page.html" target="_blank">click here</a>
```

HTML tags that use links are specific. That is, you must define the link each and every time that you link an HTML tag. So, if all your images are located in the images directory on your server, you'll need to reference the images directory each time that you link to an image; for example:

```
<img src="images/image.gif">
```

In contrast, XLink enables you to generalize. For example, you can define a base as the images directory. The base is then referenced each time you link to an image. You don't need to repeat the directory name in the link.

HTML links are limited to a one-to-one relationship between the source and destination. That is, the src attribute can reference one image file. XLink enables you to specify multiple sources with multiple destinations.

Speaking the XLink Language

Before you can begin to learn how to use XLink, you'll need to learn how to speak its language—at least to your colleagues. Let's start with the term link. A *link* defines the relationship between two or more resources, such as that between a document and an image file. A *locator* identifies the remote resource referred to in the link. And the XML element that contains the link is called the *linking element*.

Here's an example of a simple XLink:

```
<mylink xlink:type="simple" xlink:href="image.gif" xlink:show="embed" />
```

Let's identify the parts in the preceding XML code. The link element is mylink. xlink is the namespace the parser uses to identify attributes used in this statement. Each xlink is associated with an attribute.

xlink:type

The xlink:type attribute defines the type of link. There are two possible links: simple and extended.

simple

This link associates a local resource with a remote resource, which is very similar to an HTML link. A simple link is always outbound, meaning the remote resource cannot be a portion of the document that contains the xlink:type attribute.

extended

This link associates any number of resources with local or remote resources. Therefore, you use an extended type if you're referencing a resource contained within the same XML document as the xlink:type.

xline:show

xline:show specifies the presentation of the resource. There are five presentations: new, replace, embed, other, and none.

new

This causes the link to be loaded into a new window or frame; it's similar to the HTML anchor tag we show here.

```
<a href="some_page.html" target="_blank">click here</a>
```

replace
The linked resource replaces an existing resource. This is similar to an HTML link where the remote resource overwrites the document that called the remote resource.

embed
The linked resource should be inserted into the existing resource at the specified location. This is similar to an image tag in HTML.

other
This is used to enable you to define the behavior rather than depend on XLink.

none
No information is provided.

xlink:actuate

The browser evaluates links in HTML each time it encounters them while processing the XML document. In XML, links can be evaluated at specified times by specifying an attribute to the xlink:actuate element.

Four attributes are used with the xlink:actuate element: onload, onRequest, other, and none.

onload
The onload attribute specifies that the resource that's linked to the document should be loaded immediately without any user interaction. This behavior is similar to using the HTML image tag, where the image is immediately loaded and displayed within the HTML document.

onRequest
The onRequest attribute causes the linked resource to be loaded only when a specified event occurs after the XML document has been loaded. Think of the onRequest attribute as being like an HTML hyperlink where the linked HTML page isn't loaded until the web site visitor selects the hyperlink. Selecting the hyperlink is the event that triggers loading the resource.

other
The other attribute enables you to define the behavior that causes the resource to be loaded into the XML document. The behavior occurs when the parser encounters a specified tag or markup in the XML document that you specify in the attribute. This exact behavior is application defined.

none

The none attribute is used when nothing is to happen with a link. That is, the link is not used to load the resource into the XML document.

Next let's take a look at an extended link. With a simple link, you're linking to one resource much the same way you do with HTML. Here's an example of an extended link:

```
<schedule xlink:title="Jim Keogh's Courses" xlink:type="extended">
   <relation xlink:type="arc" xlink:from="student" xlink:to="course"/>
   <relation xlink:type="arc" xlink:from="student" xlink:to="counselor"/>
   <relation xlink:type="arc" xlink:from="grades"   xlink:to="student"/>
   <data xlink:type="locator" xlink:role="student"
        xlink:href="http://www.jimkeogh.com/courses/student8765.xml"/>
   <data xlink:type="locator" xlink:role="course"
      xlink:href="http://www.jimkeogh.com/courses/course9443.xml"/>
   <data xlink:type="locator" xlink:role="course"
     xlink:href="http://www.jimkeogh.com/courses/course165.xml"/>
   <data xlink:type="locator" xlink:role="course"
    xlink:href="http://www.jimkeogh.com/courses/course893.xml"/>
   <data xlink:type="locator" xlink:role="course"
     xlink:href="http://www.jimkeogh.com/courses/course786.xml"/>
   <data xlink:type="locator" xlink:role="counselor"
    xlink:href="http://www.jimkeogh/counselors/jones.xml"/>
   <grades xlink:type="resource" xlink:role="grades"
    xlink:label="grades.html">3.2</grades>
</schedule>
```

This link pulls together data from several different sources into one place. It starts by defining relationships. The student is associated with a course so the link is from the student to the course. Similarly, the student is associated with a counselor so the arc is from the student to the counselor. Grades are associated to the student so the arc is from the grades to the student. The <data> parts of link are locators to tell the processor where to find the resources. And last, the grades element pulls together the grades for the student.

XPath

Throughout this book, you've learned that an XML document is composed of many elements that are commonly referred to as *subtrees,* like branches of a tree. The parse must navigate the subtree structure in order to process the XML document. This can become a challenge in real-world XML documents because these documents are complex. You use XPath to ease the task of navigating the subtrees of an XML document.

XPath is a language that enables you to specify the location of a subtree within an XML document. The XPath language consists of declarative statements, the most important of which is the *Location Path statement*. The Location Path statement tells the parser how to locate a particular subtree.

Here's a typical Location Path statement:

```
child::class[position()<=10] / descendant::student / attribute::href
```

And here's what the Location Path statement is telling the parser. The path starts by selecting the first ten class elements of the XML document (<=10). Next, it selects all the student elements within the first ten class elements (descendant::student). And then it locates the HTML hyperlinks that are part of the first ten class elements (attribute::href).

The child::class portion of the Location Path statement selects the child elements of the document that have the name "class." That is, if the element is named "class," then the parse selects that element; otherwise the parser doesn't use the element. The position() function specifies the number of elements to select. In this case, ten child elements called class are selected. The descendant::student portion of the Location Path statement selects all the descendant elements that have the name student, which can be subtrees within the XML document.

The attribute::href specifies the name of the attribute that's being sought. This example tells the parser to look for the href attribute within the student element of the document. Table 5-1 shows commonly used XPath Location Path segments.

There are two types of Location Paths. These are *absolute path* and *relative path.* An absolute path begins with a forward slash (/), which is followed by the path that points to an element of the XML document. For example, this path starts at the root of the document and points to the student element:

/child:schedule/child:class/child:student

This would point to this element within the XML, regardless of where your current context is:

```
<schedule>
   <class>
      <student>
```

Segment	Description
Child::*	Selects all children elements of the context node
Child::text()	Selects all text node children of the context node
Child::node()	Selects all children, both elements and text nodes
attribute::*	Selects all attributes of the context node
ancestor::elementname	Selects all ancestor elements with the given name and might appear on more than one layer in the XML document

Table 5-1 Commonly Used XPath Location Path Segments

A relative path consists of a sequence of locations that are separated by a forward slash, as we show here. The path begins with an element called class and then continues within the class element to the student element.

```
child:class/child::student
```

This points to this element within the XML, assuming your current context is <schedule>.

```
<schedule>
   <class>
      <student>
```

A Closer Look at XPath

The XPath statement is divided into three parts, each separated by a forward slash, as we show here. The first part is called an *axis*. The axis specifies a tree relationship of nodes in the XML document.

```
axis_name::node_test[predicate]
```

In the following example, child is the name of the axis. The name of the element node appears after the double colon. The double colon is referred to as the *node test*. This code selects all the child nodes named "class":

```
child::class
```

This selects the four class nodes if your current context is the courses node:

```
<courses>
   <class> … </class>
   <class> … </class>
   <class> … </class>
   <class> … </class>
</courses>
```

The second part of the XPath statement is referred to as the *predicate* and begins with a forward slash. A predicate specifies a condition or restriction on the node specified in the node test. The predicate in this example is student, which is the name of a child element of class. This restricts the parser to the student element.

```
child::class/child::student
```

There are several types of axes. Table 5-2 lists commonly used axes.

Axis	Description
child	Contains the children of the context node.
descendant	Contains all children of the context node, which can go many layers deep (i.e., a child of a child of a child).
parent	Contains the parent of the context node, if there is one.
ancestor	Similar to descendant except it contains all parent nodes of the context node, including the root node of the document.
following-sibling	Contains all the following siblings of the context node. If the context node is the fourth of ten student nodes, this returns node 5 through node 10.
preceding-sibling	Contains all the preceding siblings of the context node. For example, if the context node is the fourth student node, this returns the first through the third student nodes.
following	Contains all nodes following the context node, excluding descendants, attribute nodes, and namespace nodes. Let's say the HTML head tag is the current context. This contains the body tag, but not children of the head tag or body tag.
preceding	Contains all nodes preceding the context node.
attribute	Contains the attributes of the context node. This will be empty if the context node is something other than an element.
namespace	Contains namespace nodes of the context node. This will be empty if the context node is something other than an element.
self	Contains just the context node.
descendant–or-self	Contains the context node and descendant nodes.

Table 5-2 Commonly Used Axes

Predicates

A *predicate* is a filter on a node of an XML document. Here's how this works. The parser uses the axis to select a set of nodes from the XML document. The predicate further filters the selected set of nodes.

The key to the predicate is the *proximity position.* The proximity position is the starting position of the search for the desired node. An axis is either a *forward axis,* a *reverse axis,* or a *self-axis.* A forward axis contains the context node and nodes that come after the context node. A reverse axis is an axis that contains the context node and nodes that came before the context node. A self-axis contains only itself and doesn't refer forward or backwards.

Nodes in an axis are numbered beginning with position 1 and follow in order according to where the node appears in the document. Let's say there are ten nodes in a forward axis. The first node is assigned number 1; the second is assigned number 2; and so forth.

A reverse axis reverses the order of the nodes. Consider this fragment of XML. The nodes are identified by position:

<courses>	forward axis	reverse axis
<class> … </class>	node 1	node 4
<class> … </class>	node 2	node 3
<class> … </class>	node 3	node 2
<class> … </class>	node 4	node 1
</courses>		

The predicate can be used to specify the number of each node that you want selected. Let's say that you want node 1 through and including node 5. Here's the location statement that you need to write:

```
child::class[position()<=5]
```

The predicate is position() <=5. This states that you want to select node 1 through and including node 5. The predicate returns a Boolean value—true or false. A false is returned if a node doesn't meet the predicate filter; otherwise, a true is returned.

A predicate can specify a specific value. Let's say that you want to select the node called name, whose value is Mary Smith. Here's how you write this statement. This says to select the student nodes that have a child element called name with a text value of Mary Smith:

```
child::student[child::name='Mary Smith']
```

You can also use predicates to match attributes of an element. Suppose you want to match the student ID 123. The student ID is assigned to the id attribute. Here's the statement that you need to write. This says to select the student element nodes that have an id attribute with a value of 123.

```
Child::student[attribute::id='123']
```

Functions

By now, you probably guessed that XPath uses functions (since you used the position() function in a previous example). Functions play an important role in writing predicates because you can use them to perform a task where the results of the task determine the filter value for the predicate.

For example, you used the position() function to return the position of the current node in a node set. Once you know the position, the predicate expression uses the position to determine if the node should be selected.

Table 5-3 contains commonly used XPath functions.

Position Functions	**Description**
number position()	Returns the position of a node within a node set.
number last()	Returns the position of the last node in the node set. This can be used to either get the last node or return the size of the node set.
number count(node-set)	Similar to last() except you pass a node set as an argument. This can be used to evaluate any node set where last() only looks at the current context node.
node-set id(object)	If the argument object is a node set, this returns a node set that represents the union of all nodes that have an id equal to one of the nodes passed in as an argument. If the argument is a string, the string is parsed into tokens separated by white space, and then it returns a node set where each node has an id equal to one of the tokens.
String Functions	**Description**
string string(object)	Converts the object argument into a string.
string concat(string, string, string*)	Returns the concatenation of the arguments.
boolean starts-with(string, string)	Returns true if the first argument string starts with the second argument string; otherwise, it returns false.
boolean contains(string, string)	Returns true if the first argument string contains the second argument string; otherwise, it returns false.
string substring-before(string, string)	Returns the substring of the first argument string that precedes the first occurrence of the second argument string in the first argument string, or returns the empty string if the first argument string doesn't contain the second argument string.
string substring-after(string, string) -	Returns the substring of the first argument string that follows the first occurrence of the second argument string in the first argument string, or returns the empty string if the first argument string doesn't contain the second argument string.

Table 5-3 Commonly Used XPath Functions

String Functions	Description
string substring(string, number, number?)	Returns the substring of the first argument starting at the position specified by the second argument. The third argument is optional and specifies the maximum number of characters to include in the returned substring. Position 1 is the first character in the string. This is different than it is with languages such as C and Java, where the first position is 0.
number string-length(string?)	Returns the number of characters in the string. Notice that the argument is optional. If the argument is omitted, the function defaults to the context node and the context node is converted to a string and returned.
Boolean Functions	**Description**
boolean boolean(object)	This function depends on the type of argument as follows: A number is true if it is not zero and not NaN (not a number). A string is true if its length is greater than zero. A node set is true if its size is greater than zero. An object is converted to a Boolean in a way that's dependent on the type of object.
boolean not(boolean)	Returns true if the argument is false; otherwise, it returns false.
boolean true()	Always returns true.
boolean false()	Always returns false.
boolean lang(string)	Returns true if the language of the context node is the same as the argument of a sublanguage of the argument. The language is specified in the xml::lang attribute of the context node.
Number Functions	**Description**
number number(object?)	Converts the argument to a number. This depends on the type of argument passed as follows: A string will be converted to a number provided the string contains only an optional + or – sign followed by digits. Whitespace is permitted on either side of the string but any other characters will cause this to return NaN. A Boolean argument of true will return 1 and a Boolean false will return 0.

Table 5-3 Commonly Used XPath Functions *(continued)*

Number Functions	Description
number sum(node-set)	Returns the sum of the node set by converting each node in the node set to a number.
number floor(number)	Returns the closest integer less than or equal to the argument; for example, floor(4.6) returns 4 and floor(–9.7) returns –10.
number ceiling(number)	Returns the closest integer greater than or equal to the argument; for example, ceiling(4.6) return 5 and ceiling(–9.7) returns –9.
number round(number)	Returns the closest integer to the argument. The function "rounds up"; in other words, round(4.5) returns 5 and round(–4.5) returns –4. If the argument is NaN, then it returns NaN.

Table 5-3 Commonly Used XPath Functions *(continued)*

XPointer

XLink uses XPointer to identify the location of a resource, even if the document doesn't contain any anchor elements. This means that you can change the linked resource without changing the links to that resource.

Here's how XPointer works. Let's say that you want to reference the second resource of the following resource. Here's the XPointer statement that you'll need to write. The # symbol is the XPointer and it tells the parser to go to the first ten students of the class element in the page.html resource. This code says to go to the class element and link to the first ten student elements:

```
http://www.foo.org/page.html#xpointer(class/student[position <= 10])
```

In HTML you define an anchor id and link directly to the anchor tag. The XPointer example lets you do this and lets you link to multiple nodes within the same document.

Looking Ahead

In this chapter you learned how you use XLink, XPath, and XPointer to link to outside resources and to navigate an XML document. XLink is similar to links used in an HTML document to access HTML pages, images, and other resources that are not included in the HTML document. However, XLink can link to multiple resources, depending on the behavior of an element with an XML document.

XPath is a language used to specify a subtree within an XML document. The Location Path statement is the most important component of XPath because it tells the parser how to locate a particular subtree in the document. The Location Path statement uses a predicate that contains the criteria for selecting the subtree. You use XPath functions and logical operators to write the expression that specifies the selection criteria.

XPointer identifies the location of a resource, even if the document doesn't contain any anchor elements; this enables you to change the linked resource without changing the links to that resource.

Quiz

1. A locator identifies the remote resource referred to in the link.
   a. True
   b. False
2. A simple link
   a. Associates a local resource with a remote resource
   b. Associates any number of resources with local or remote resources
   c. Associates an xlink:type with an XML document
   d. None of the above
3. xline:new
   a. Enables you to define the linking behavior
   b. Inserts a resource into the existing resource
   c. Overwrites an existing resource
   d. Is the link to be loaded into a new window or frame
4. In XML, links can be evaluated
   a. Only when the link is encountered
   b. At specified times, by specifying an attribute to the xlink:actuate element
   c. Only when the link is loaded
   d. Immediately before the link is read by the parser

5. onRequest is similar to
   a. An HTML hyperlink
   b. An HTML image link
   c. An HTML body tag
   d. An HTML head tag
6. XPath specifies an external resource.
   a. True
   b. False
7. A predicate is used with XPointer to establish selection criteria.
   a. True
   b. False
8. In child::class, class is
   a. The name of the element
   b. The name of a function
   c. The name of the XML document
   d. None of the above
9. An axis called attributes contains nodes called attribute nodes.
   a. True
   b. False
10. The position() function is used to determine an element's position in an XML document.
    a. True
    b. False

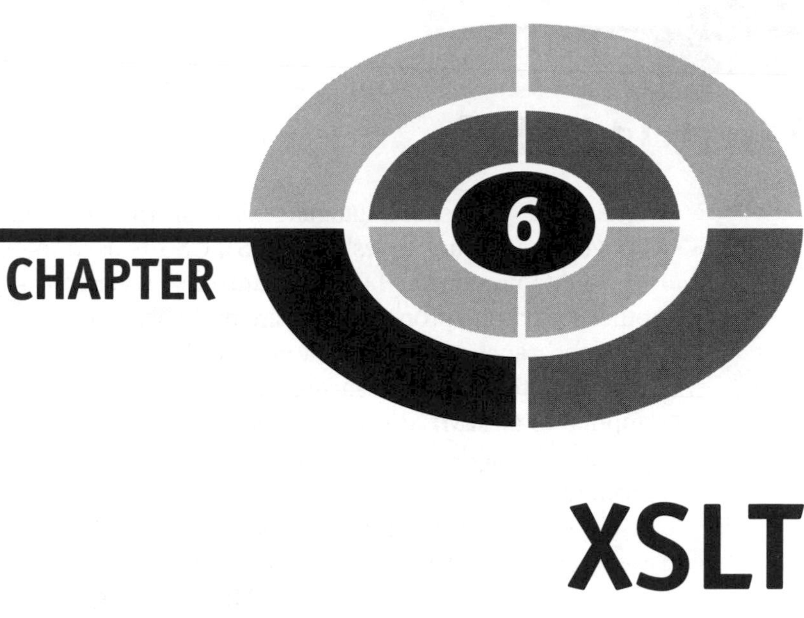

XSLT

You've probably heard of the difficulties federal law enforcement agencies have sharing electronic data. Data is stored in different formats, which can prevent one agency's computers from reading another agency's data.

This is a common problem anyone who works with data faces. However, you can resolve much of this problem by using XML. You feel the true power of XML when you use it to efficiently convert text in an XML document into a different format that any application can access. The conversion process is called *transformation,* and if the XML document is associated with a stylesheet, a processor handles the conversion.

A *stylesheet* is a road map that shows an application how to convert the XML document into another format. In this chapter, you'll learn how to create a stylesheet and how to use an XSLT processor to transform an XML document into an entirely different format.

What Is XSLT?

Extensible Stylesheet Language Transformation (XSLT) is XML's version of HTML's cascading stylesheet (CSS). CSS is used to describe the style that should be used to present an HTML document. A style consists of fonts, colors, sizes, and other formatting properties that are probably familiar to you if you've ever changed the appearance of a document in a word processor.

The Extensible Stylesheet Language (XSL) describes the style that should be applied to an XML document, and XSLT is the process, called *transforming,* that applies the style to the XML document. This transformation sets XSLT apart from CSS.

CSS describes the finer details of how the HTML document will appear on the web page. XSL describes the new format of an XML document, such as an HTML document, Extensible Hypertext Markup Language (XHTML) document, or any format that an application requires. XSTL converts the XML document to the new format according to instructions in the XSL.

Think of XSLT as the key to making an XML document come alive. As you'll recall from Chapter 1, an XML document contains markup tags that aren't readable by a browser or other software because XML markup tags are customized by the developer. That is, the browser doesn't know the difference between text and an XML markup tag.

However, the browser understands HTML and XHTML markup tags because they've been standardized. XSLT bridges the communication gap by transforming an XML document into a format that's readable by a browser or other software.

XPath and the Transformation

An XML document is typically organized into sections, each one containing data. For example, a customers section identified by the customers XML markup tag contains one or more customers, each one identified by the customer XML markup tag. There might be hundreds of customer sections within a customers section in a real-world XML document.

Let's say that a request is made to display information about a particular customer on a web page. In order to do this, the XML document must be transformed into an HTML document before the browser can display the customer's information.

Instead of transforming the entire XML document into an HTML document, XSLT uses XPath (see Chapter 5) to locate information about a particular customer in the XML document. You'll recall that the XPath feature enables you to navigate through an XML document, skipping over unneeded elements and reading only those elements that need to be extracted. Once it's found, only the customer's information is transformed into the HTML document and sent to the browser. Other parts of the XML document remain untouched.

Source and Result Documents

XSLT references two documents. These are called the *source document* and the *result document.* The source document is the XML document that's being transformed. The result document is the target file, such as an HTML document.

It's important to realize that a result document can be any format your application requires. Typically this is an HTML or XHTML document. However, you can transform an XML document into a format that's specific to any application software.

Think of XSLT as basically the search and replace feature found in most word processors. XSL identifies the pattern of characters XSLT must search for in the source document. XSL also identifies the pattern of characters that XSLT must write in the result when these characters are found. This enables you to transform an XML document into any document.

For example, the XSL might say if customerFirstName is found in the source document, then write <h3> <cTypeface:Bold>, then the customer's first name followed by </b></h3> in the result document.

XSLT in Action

Now that you have a good understanding of what XSLT is and how it generally works, you can create your own XSL. However, before doing so you'll need to have an environment to test your creations in.

Many popular web browsers, such as Netscape 8.0 and Internet Explorer 6.0, have XSLT support. Make sure you have one of these browsers installed on your computer. If you don't, then download the latest browser from www.netscape.com, www.microsoft.com, or from any web site that offers a downloadable browser with support for XSLT.

You're ready to write your first XSLT once you have an XSLT-supported browser installed on your computer. Let's begin by creating an XML source document. Use a text editor and write the following XML document, then save it in a file called customers.xml.

```
<?xml version="1.0"?>
<?xml-stylesheet type="text/xsl" href="customers.xsl"?>
<customers>
  <customer id="286">
    <firstname>Henry</firstname>
    <lastname>Hudson</lastname>
    <phone>
      <areacode>212</areacode>
      <exchange>555</exchange>
      <number>5576</number>
    </phone>
  </customer>
  <customer id="588">
    <firstname>Jim</firstname>
    <lastname>Keogh</lastname>
    <phone/>
  </customer>
</customers>
```

Next you'll write the XSL stylesheet. Using the text editor, write the following stylesheet and save it to a file called customers.xsl. Make sure that this file is in the same directory as the customers.xml file.

```
<?xml version="1.0"?>
<xsl:stylesheet version="1.0"
       xmlns:xsl="http://www.w3.org/1999/XSL/Transform">
<xsl:template match="/">
  <html>
  <body>
    <h2>Customer Listing</h2>
    <table border="1">
    <tr>
      <th align="center">Customer ID</th>
      <th align="center">Name</th>
    </tr>
    <xsl:for-each select="customers/customer">
    <tr>
      <td>
         <xsl:value-of select="@id"/>
      </td>
```

```
        <td>
          <xsl:value-of select="firstname"/> 
          <xsl:value-of select="lastname"/>
        </td>
      </tr>
      </xsl:for-each>
      </table>
    </body>
    </html>
</xsl:template>
</xsl:stylesheet>
```

Open the customers.xml document using an XSLT-supported browser. When the browser encounters the following line in the customers.xml document, it opens the XSL file. Here it finds instructions on how to transform the customers.xml document into an HTML document, which is the result file. Once the document is transformed, the browser reads the HTML tags and displays the result file on the screen: <?xml-stylesheet type="text/xsl" href="customers.xsl"?>

The result document looks something like the following customer listing when it's displayed by the browser.

Customer ID	Name
286	Henry Hudson
588	Jim Keogh

The result document is XHTML, which is displayed as a regular HTML document. When you view the source, you'll see the XML document. The resulting XHTML is displayed in the browser.

A Closer Look at XSL Stylesheet

The XSL stylesheet contains a mixture of XSL and HTML. You can probably pick out the HTML tags and have a good idea of how the HTML tags are used in the result document if you view the source code in the browser.

Let's take a closer look at the XSL stylesheet. The XSL stylesheet begins with the XML declaration that identifies the version of XML that's being used in the source document:

```
<?xml version="1.0"?>
```

Next, you define the version of XSL that's used for the XSL stylesheet:

```
<xsl:stylesheet version="1.0" xmlns:xsl="http://www.w3.org/1999/XSL/Transform">
```

Style instructions, such as </xsl:for-each>, follow these declarations. The instructions are

- <xsl:template>
- <xsl:value-of>
- <xsl:for-each>
- <xsl:if>
- <xsl:choose>
- <xsl:sort>
- <xsl:apply-templates>

<xsl:template>

An XSL stylesheet contains a set of rules that XSLT uses to transform the source document into the result document. These rules are based on matching templates. This simply tells XSLT to search for a particular pattern of characters in the source document.

The <xsl:template> element is used for matching. The pattern of characters that are to be matched is assigned to the match attribute. The match attribute in the previous example is assigned / , as we show here:

```
<xsl:template match="/">
```

The / implies matching the root element, which means matching the entire source document. The root element is an entry point into the source document and not part of the source document itself. From the root, the first child is the <customers> element.

Let's take a closer look at the follow snippet of the XSL stylesheet to get a better understanding of the role of the root element:

```
<xsl:template match="/">
...
     <xsl:for-each select="customers/customer">
    ...
    </xsl:for-each>
 ...
</xsl:template>
```

You start by matching the root of the document and then move to the <xsl:for-each> element. The <xsl:for-each> element iterates the customer elements as

instructed by the value of the select attribute. The select attribute customers/customer refers to the customer element, which is the child of the customers element.

The <xsl:for-each> element says, "For each occurrence of the customer element within the customers element." You can achieve the same result by using the following code. The match attribute states, "Begin at the root (entry point of the source document) and go to the customers element."

```
<xsl:template match="/customers">
...
     <xsl:for-each select="customer">
    ...
    </xsl:for-each>
  ...
</xsl:template>
```

<xsl:value-of>

The <xsl:value-of> element extracts text from the source document and transforms it into the result document. This is the XPath. In the example we show you in the previous section, we're extracting the customer ID and the customer's first and last names.

The <xsl:value-of select="@id"/> instruction extracts the customer ID. The @ symbol indicates that the customer ID is an attribute of the customer element and not a child element.

The <xsl:value-of select="firstname"/> instruction extracts the customer's first name which is contained in the firstname element of the source document. You're probably wondering if   is a typo. It isn't.

This is a whitespace that's inserted into the result document, so there's a space between the customer's first and last names. 160 is the ISO-8859-1 character value for a nonbreaking whitespace character, which is the equivalent of   in HTML. (ISO is the International Standards Organization that among other things establishes values for various nonprintable characters such as a space.)

We're retrieving all customers from the source document in our example. In a real-world application, you might need to retrieve a particular customer. You can do this by modifying the attribute value of <xsl:value-of select="@id"/>.

Suppose you want only customer 286. Here's what you need to write:

```
<xsl:value-of select="@id='286'"/>
```

Likewise, you can specify values for XML elements, such as the first name of a customer as we show here:

```
<xsl:for-each select="firstname='Jim'">
```

<xsl:for-each>

The <xsl:for-each> element defines what is to happen when the XLST encounters each customer element in the source XML document. Two things will happen. XLST writes a new row and two columns in HTML format to the result document. XLST also extracts the customer ID and the customer's first and last names from the XML document and writes them into the appropriate columns in each row.

HTML elements are placed within the <xsl:for-each> element just as you write them into an HTML document. You use the <xsl:value-of select=/> element to extract text from the source document. Place the <xsl:value-of select=/> element wherever you want the text to appear in the HTML document. In this example, we're placing it within the <td> element.

It's important to keep in mind that you can replace the HTML format with any format that your application requires.

<xsl:if>

XSL supports conditional logic by using the <xsl:if> element. The <xsl:if> element uses a test attribute to specify if an action should be taken. The value of the test attribute is a conditional expression.

Let's say that want to display a message if the customer's first name is Jim. Here's what you'd write. XSLT writes <p>Hello Jim!</p> into the result document whenever it encounters Jim as the text for the <firstname> element in the XML source document.

```
<xsl:if test="firstname='Jim'">
   <p>Hello Jim!</p>
</xsl:if>
```

<xsl:choose>

The <xsl:choose> element tells XSLT to choose one or more lines to write to the result document based on a test condition. The <xsl:choose> element contains two or more <xsl:when test=> elements, which contain a test attribute whose value is a conditional expression that determines if lines within the <xsl:when test=> element should be written to the result document. The <xsl:choose> element can also contain the <xsl:otherwise> element, which contains lines that are to be written to the result document if none of the <xsl:when test=> element conditions are met.

The following code illustrates how this works. This example compares the firstname element text of the XML source document to Jim and to Bob. If either matches the text of the firstname element, then the appropriate Hello message is written to the result document. If neither matches, then the Hello message within the <xsl:otherwise> element is written to the result document.

```
<xsl:choose>
   <xsl:when test="firstname='Jim'">
      <p>Hello Jim!</p>
   </xsl:when>
   <xsl:when test="firstname='Bob'">
      <p>Hello Bob!</p>
   </xsl:when>
   <xsl:otherwise>
      <p>Hello!</p>
   </xsl:otherwise>
</xsl:choose>
```

<xsl:sort>

Text extracted from the XML source document can be written to the result document in sorted order by using the <xsl:sort> element in the XST stylesheet. The sort is based on the value of the select attribute of the <xsl:sort> element.

For example, here's how you sort the text of the lastname element in the XML source document. The <xsl:sort> element must appear as the first element within the <xsl:for-each> element.

```
<xsl:sort select="lastname"/>
```

XSL sorts in natural order and is *case insensitive*. This means uppercase and lowercase versions of the same letter appear in the same location of the sorted document. You can specify if the uppercase or the lowercase version of the same letter appears first using the case-order attribute of the <xsl:sort> tag, as we show here. Lower-first means that the lowercase version of the letter appears before the uppercase version of the same letter, and upper-first places the uppercase version first.

```
<xsl:sort select="lastname" case-order="lower-first"/>
<xsl:sort select="lastname" case-order="upper-first"/>
```

The default sort order is ascending; however, you can change the sort order to descending by setting the order attribute to descending, as we illustrate here:

```
<xsl:sort select="lastname" order="descending"/>
```

Sorting can be tricky when the element contains a number rather than letters. Numbers are treated as text. This means that

1
2
10

is sorted as

1
10
2

You really want this sorted in numerical order. You can fix this problem by using the data-type attribute of the <xsl:sort> element. Set the data-type attribute to number and XSLT places the numbers in numerical order, as we show here:

```
<xsl:sort select="@id" data-type="number"/>
```

<xsl:apply-templates>

Writing an XSL can become time-consuming, especially if you have to define styles for many elements in an XML source document. A common problem you might run into is replicating lines of code when you want to repeat a style element in the XSL stylesheet.

You can avoid replicating code by creating a *template.* A template associates a block of code with a name. You use the name in your XSL stylesheet whenever you want the block of code to appear in the XSL stylesheet.

You create the template using the <xsl:templates> element. Let's suppose that an XML source document describes a telephone number using the areacode element, exchange element, and number element. You'll need to reference each of these every time you want to extract a telephone number.

Instead of repeating these, you can create a template and then call the template whenever you want to extract elements of the phone number. Here's how to create a template. The value of the match attribute is the name of the template.

```
<xsl:template match="phone">
   (<xsl:value-of select="areacode"/>)
   <xsl:value-of select="exchange"/> -
   <xsl:value-of select="number"/>
</xsl:template>
```

You call the template by using the <xsl:apply-templates> element in the XSL stylesheet, as we show here. The value of the select attribute is the name of the template that you want to use.

```
<td>
   <xsl:apply-templates select="phone"/>
</td>
```

Looking Ahead

You use the Extensible Stylesheet Language (XSL) to describe how an XML document is to be transformed by the Extensible Stylesheet Language Transformation (XSLT) processor into a result document. Transformation is the process of converting an XML document into another format that includes HTML and XHTML. XSLT uses XPath to locate portions of an XML document that need to be transformed into the result document.

The XSL stylesheet contains a blend of XSL instructions and characters that, together, form a result document, which then is accessible to another application such as a browser. You begin the XSL stylesheet by defining the versions of XML and XSL that are being used. You then follow with a definition of a template.

The template contains XSL instructions that perform various operations on the XML document. The <xsl:for-each> instruction executes one or more additional instructions for each XML element that's specified in the <xsl:for-each> instruction.

The <xsl:value-of/> instruction extracts text from a specified element in the XML document and writes it to the result document. The <xsl:if> instruction causes the XSLT processor to evaluate a condition in the XML document. If the condition exists, then lines within the <xsl:if> instruction are copied to the result document.

The <xsl:choose> instruction requires the processor to evaluate several conditions in the XML document and then copy lines within the <xsl:then> portion of the <xsl: choose> instruction to the result document.

You can sort text extracted from the source document by using the <xsl:sort> instruction. This instruction places the text in natural ascending order. There are attributes you can use to change the natural order.

A block of XSL instructions can be associated with a name and then used elsewhere in the XSL stylesheet by simply referring to that name.

Quiz

1. XML can only be transformed into HTML or XHTML.
   a. True
   b. False
2. Instructions for transforming an XML document are contained in the
   a. XSL stylesheet
   b. CSS stylesheet
   c. XSLT stylesheet
   d. None of the above
3. The <xsl:for-each select="customers/customer"> statement states
   a. For each customer element of the result document
   b. For each customers element of the result document

c. For each customer element of the source document that's a child of customers

d. For each customers element of the source document

4. The <xsl:value-of> element is used to

a. Extract text from the result document

b. Extract text from the source document

c. Place text into the source document

d. None of the above

5. The <xsl:value-of select="@id='Jim'"/> statement is used to

a. Select the Jim element

b. Select the id attribute

c. Select the Jim attribute

d. Select the id attribute if the value is 'Jim'

6. The <xsl:for-each> element contains only XSL elements.

a. True

b. False

7. The <xsl:if> element instructs the CSS to evaluate a condition before extracting an element.

a. True

b. False

8. In order to sort numeric values, you must set the <xsl:sort> to

a. data-type="number"

b. data-type="value"

c. data-type="decimal"

d. None of the above

9. You can repeat lines of code within the XSL stylesheet by defining an apply-template.

a. True

b. False

10. Only a browser can access a result document.

a. True

b. False

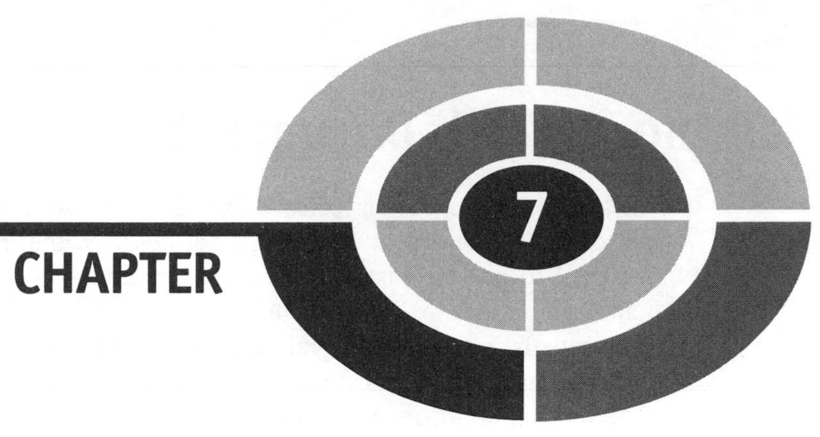

XML Parsers and Transformations

A parser is the powerhouse that makes an XML document come alive and become a universal way to exchange information among different applications. It can transform a bunch of characters in an XML document into anything you can imagine.

There are many parsers that you can choose from but each conforms to one of two standards: the Simple API for XML (SAX) and Document Object Model (DOM). There is also the Java Transformer, which enables you to translate between DOM, SAX, and a stream. Your job is to choose the standard that's right for your job.

In this chapter, we provide you with insight into each standard, enabling you to make an intelligence choice when selecting a parser to transform your XML documents.

Parsing an XML Document

An XML document is basically a text file where some tags represent information and other tags represent XML tags that describe the information. XML tags are designed to provide instructions to the program that transforms the information contained in the XML document into another form. The program that reads and interprets the information is called a *parser* and the process where information in an XML document is transformed into another form is called *transformation.*

In its simplest form, a parser extracts and reformats information contained in an XML document based on the XML tag that describes the information. For example, suppose that the parser encountered the <CustomerLastName> XML tag. The parser copies information contained in the tag and then reformats it into an HTML document. The parser reads it, and the transformer allows you to convert it to another type of document; for example, an HTML document.

In its more complicated form, a parser extracts selected XML tags and reformats the information based on business logic. Suppose account manager Bob Smith is planning a sales trip and wants a list of the customers who are within the same vicinity. The list can be generated by giving the parser specific instructions, such as search the XML document for customers whose account manager is Bob Smith. Once they're found, the parser determines if the customer's zip code is within a specific set of zip codes. If so, then select information about the customer is copied from the XML document into an HTML web page that is displayed on Bob Smith's computer.

Instructions for the parser are written in the Extensible Stylesheet Language Transformation (XSLT) and stored in the Extensible Stylesheet Language (XSL), which you learned about in the Chapter 6.

A parser is a program. There are a number of parsers that are available, each of which adheres to one of two XML parsing standards. These standards are SAX and DOM.

The Simple API for XML (SAX)

The Simple API for XML (SAX) standard was developed by members of the XML-DEV mailing list. It was driven by a need to have an open standard for companies or public organizations; this way, they could implement a standard that would be consistent across the board.

SAX is not technically an XML parser—it's a specification that defines the interface to the parser. Its first release was in May 1998. Of all the implementations of the SAX specification, the Java implementation is probably the most mature and most widely used.

It's important to understand that SAX is a standard for an application program interface (API). It specifies standards for classes that you use to build a SAX parser.

This may sound confusing, especially if you've never programmed before. However, you can probably imagine the many steps that are necessary to read and transform an XML document. You need to write code for each step in order to build a parser to transform the XML documents. This is a tedious and time-consuming job.

However, you can minimize the tedium and save time by using the classes of an API, which other developers have already written. Think of these classes as already assembled subparts of the parser. You assemble the subparts together to create a parser.

You aren't expected to write a parser, but you'll need a parser in order to transform your XML document. A SAX parser (a parser that was developed using the SAX API) is designed to read large XML documents because it starts at the beginning of the XML document and reads a group of lines, called *a block at a time,* until it reaches the end of the document. The entire transformation process occurs in one reading.

As it reads each block, the SAX parser determines if the block contains an XML tag or information. If it's an XML tag, the SAX parser compares the XML tag to the XSL and then transforms the information based on the XSL instructions. The SAX parser then reads the next block of the XML document.

A block is discarded once it's transformed. This frees memory for the next block, which gives the SAX parser an advantage over a DOM parser. A DOM parser loads the entire XML document in memory, which you'll learn about in "The Document Object Model," later in this chapter. The SAX parser requires a small amount of memory to transform a very large XML document.

This advantage is also a disadvantage because a SAX parser cannot reference a block of an XML document other than the block that's in memory. This means that it cannot modify XML information that has already been transformed based on the block that's currently being read.

A SAX parser gets one chance at reading each XML tag. Sometimes this is all you need, though for a more complex transformation, you'll need to use a DOM parser that can reference any part of the XML document (see "The Document Object Model," later in this chapter).

Components of a SAX Parser

There are four components in a SAX parser: the *Content Handler, Error Handler, DTD Handler,* and *Entity Resolver.*

The Content Handler is responsible for reacting to events that occur during the transformation of the XML document. An *event* is something that happens while the SAX parser reads the XML document, such as starting the document, starting an element, ending a document, and ending an element. Table 7-1 lists some of the events in the order that they occur when the SAX parser transforms an XML document.

Each event is associated with a method. A *method* is a block of instructions that's executed whenever the event occurs while the XML document is being parsed. For example, instructions in the startDocument() method are executed when the parser begins to parse the XML document.

This can be seen in the following example. It's a short XML document, but it contains all the components that are necessary to illustrate how a SAX parser works. The first event that occurs is starting to parse the XML document. This results in calling the startDocument().

The next event is starting an element, which is the <customer> element. The startElement() method is called. Another start element event happens when the <firstname> is read. This is followed by a character event that triggers the characters() method to execute, and is when the information within the <firstname> tag is copied and transformed according the XSL. The close element event is next when the </firstname> tag is read. This causes the endElement() method to run. This pattern continues until the XML parser reads the last element. The last event is the end of the document, which causes the endDocument() method to execute. As you can see, writing an application that uses the SAX parser can get complicated. You need to keep track of where you are in the document to extract the data you're interested in.

```
<?xml version="1.0"?>
<customer>
  <firstname>Jim</firstname>
  <lastname>Keogh</lastname>
</customer>
```

Event	Description
startDocument()	Start parsing
startElement()	Element opening tag
characters()	Information in the element
endElement()	Element closing tag
endDocument()	End parsing

Table 7-1 Events That Occur When Parsing an XML Document

The Error Handler is the component of a SAX parser that responds to errors discovered by the SAX parser when it's reading the XML document. There are three types of errors: *warnings, error,* and *fatal error.*

A warning indicates that the SAX parser encountered something unusual in the XML document, but it wasn't enough to stop it from transforming the XML document. An error is more serious than a warning. It doesn't prevent the parser from continuing; however, the transformed document might be properly transformed. A fatal error prevents the SAX parser from continuing.

Each error has a corresponding error handler that's called when the SAX parser encounters it. A handler is a method with instructions on how to respond to the error. These methods are warning(), error(), and fatalError().

You don't need to be concerned with how error handlers work. However, you do need to understand how to react to the error messages that these error handlers display. Each SAX parser has its own set of error messages, so you'll need to refer to the documentation that comes with your SAX parser to know how to respond to error messages.

The DTD Handler

The DTD Handler reads the Data Type Definition (DTD) (see Chapter 3) and then uses the DTD to validate tags in the XML document. If an XML tag violates the DTD, the DTD Handler causes the Error Handler to display a warning or error message on the screen indicating the nature of the problem. We illustrate this in the following XML document and DTD.

The XML document:

```
<?xml version="1.0"?>
<!DOCTYPE customer SYSTEM "customer.dtd">
<customer id="123" type="manufacturing">
  <firstname>Jim</firstname>
  <lastname>Keogh</lastname>
</customer>
```

The DTD:

```
<!ELEMENT customer (firstname, lastname)>
<!ELEMENT firstname (#PCDATA)>
<!ELEMENT lastname (#PCDATA)>
<!ATTLIST customer
   id (CDATA) #REQUIRED
   type (retail|wholesale) "retail">
```

Notice the XML is properly formed; however, there's a mistake in the customer type attribute. The DTD provides the allowable values of "retail" or "wholesale." If the attribute isn't present in the XML, the customer type attribute defaults to "retail," according to the DTD. The XML has a value of "manufacturing." This produces a warning in the XML document, but it doesn't prevent the XML from being parsed because it's still properly formed XML.

Try changing the customer tag to:

```
<customer id="123" type=manufacturing">
```

This will produce a fatal error. There's no quotation mark after type=. This type of error prevents the XML from parsing correctly.

The Entity Resolver component of the SAX parser helps the SAX parser locate external resources that are referenced within the XML document. Oftentimes, an XML document contains references to the URL of an external resource, such as the location of the DTD.

The URL is referenced in the XML document, but additional information related to the resource is contained in the Entity Resolver.

Suppose you have this DOCTYPE declaration in your XML document:

```
<!DOCTYPE web-app
   PUBLIC "-//My Company, Inc.//DTD Web Application"
   "http://www.jimkeogh.com/dtds/web-app.dtd">
```

The DTD is located at http://www.jimkeogh.com/dtds/web-app.dtd. Your application may be running on a server that doesn't have access to the Internet so you won't be able to get a copy of the DTD. This is one place where you can use an Entity Resolver. The parser calls your Entity Resolver when it encounters this DOCTYPE tag. You can then direct it to a location where it can find it. You can put a copy on the local file system or another server that you do have access to. This, in effect, overrides the default behavior. It's a means of telling the parser where to find these external resources. You may not have the option of modifying the original XML to point to a more convenient location, so you can use the Entity Resolver to deal with it.

The Document Object Model

The Document Object Model (DOM) is similar to SAX in that it's a standard that defines an API used by the developer to create a parser. However, a DOM parser works differently than a SAX parser because a DOM parser reads the entire XML document, organizes the XML document into a tree structure, and stores it into memory.

The DOM parser uses the tree structure to access parts of the XML document without having to read the XML document sequentially (from top to bottom), as is the case with the SAX parser. This means that a DOM parser can refer back to a previously read portion of the XML document, which is a disadvantage of using the SAX parser.

The DOM parser is also capable of creating an XML document and altering an existing XML document, something that cannot be done if you use a SAX parser because a SAX parser cannot write an XML document. It is read only.

However, the DOM parser has a major disadvantage in that it can only read XML documents that can fit into memory, which makes the DOM parser an unlikely choice if you need to transform very large XML documents. The available memory in the computer that runs the DOM parser must be sufficient to store the XML document; otherwise you won't be able to use the DOM parser.

Here's how the DOM parser works. Suppose you want to parse the following XML document. Obviously it will fit into memory, so you can use a DOM parser. Figure 7-1 shows the tree structure that the DOM parser builds in memory.

```
<?xml version="1.0"?>
<customer>
  <firstname>Jim</firstname>
  <lastname>Keogh</lastname>
</customer>
```

The root is the beginning of the XML document and extends to *nodes*. A node is like a branch of the tree. The first node is an element node that contains the customer element. Compare Figure 7-1 to the XML document and you'll see how the tree follows along with the structure of the XML document.

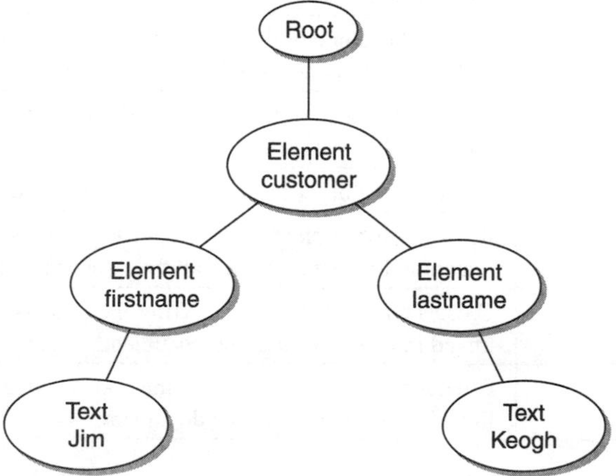

Figure 7-1 The DOM parser builds a tree structure of the XML document in memory.

The customer element in the XML document contains the firstname and lastname elements. The firstname element contains the information Jim and the lastname element contains the information Keogh. These are represented as text nodes in the tree. A real-world XML document will probably have comments and Character Data (CDATA) sections. Each of these is represented as a node on the tree by the DOM parser. Processing instructions are not part of the DOM tree.

The DOM API provides a variety of methods that you can use to build the DOM parser. Table 7-2 lists some methods used to navigate the tree structure of the XML document. You don't need to use them, but it gives you insight into how the DOM parser can move about the tree.

Method	Description
getFirstChild()	Returns the first child node, such as customer node in Figure 7-1.
getLastChild()	Returns the last child node. If customer is the current node, then lastname is the last child node.
getChildNodes()	Returns a list of child nodes in the order they appear in the document. If customer is the current node, then the list of child notes contains firstname and lastname.
getNextSibling()	Returns the sibling that's right of the current node at the same node level. If firstname is the current node, the next sibling is lastname.
getPreviousSibling()	Returns the sibling that's left of the current node at the same node level. If lastname is the current node, the next sibling is firstname.
getParentNode()	Returns the parent node of the current node. If firstname is the current node, then customer is returned.
getNodeType()	Returns the type of the current node. If firstname is the current node, then element node is returned.
getNodeName()	Returns the name of the current node. If customer is the current node, then the name customer is returned.
getNodeValue()	Returns the value of the current node. If Text Jim is the current node, the Jim is returned.
getAttributes()	Returns a list of attributes that are defined in the current node.
getElementsByTagName()	Returns a list of elements that have the same name. If you're searching for lastname, then all the lastname elements are returned.
createElement()	Creates a new element node. After the node is created, it can be linked into any place in the document.
createTextNode()	Creates a new text node. After the node is created, it can be linked into any place in the document.

Table 7-2 Methods in the DOM API

Method	Description
createComment()	Creates a new comment node. After the node is created, it can be linked into any place in the document.
appendChild()	Links a new child node to the current node.
insertBefore()	Inserts a node into a specific location within the tree.

Table 7-2 Methods in the DOM API *(continued)*

Let's see how a DOM parser updates the tree of an XML document. Once updated, the tree is then transformed back to an XML document. Here's the updated document. Notice that we inserted a middlename element within the customer element:

```
<?xml version="1.0"?>
<customer>
  <firstname>Jim</firstname>
  <middlename>Edward</middlename>
  <lastname>Keogh</lastname>
</customer>
```

Now you want to reflect this change in the tree as shown in Figure 7-2. To do this, the createElement() method is called to create the middlename element and then the insertBefore() method is called to place the middlename element before the lastname element in the tree.

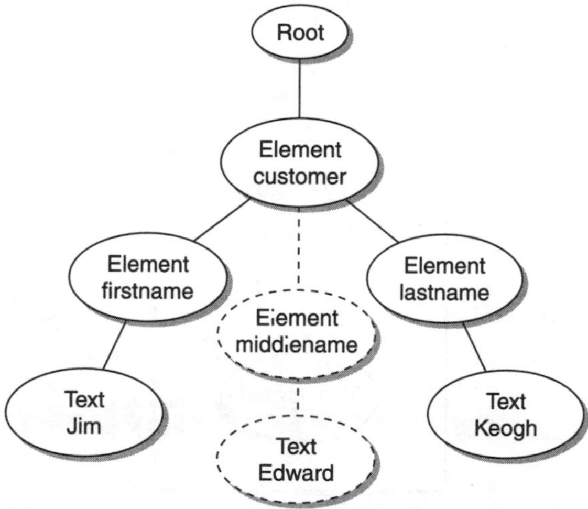

Figure 7-2 The middlename element and text are inserted into the tree.

The getPreviousSibling() method is called next to move to the middlename element, which is previous to the lastname element. The createTextNode()method is called to create a text node that contains the name Edward. The appendChild() method is then called to place the new text node beneath the middlename element in the tree.

***TIP** Sometimes when running a DOM parser, you'll see an error message referring to the SAX parser. This can be confusing since you're not running a SAX parser. Well, that isn't totally true. The DOM parser initially uses a SAX parser to read the XML file. Errors that occur during the initial parsing are SAX parser errors and not DOM parser errors.*

Java and Parsing an XML Document

Java is a popular programming language used to develop applications that can run on different kinds of computers without having to rewrite the program. That is, the same physical program can run on computers that run Windows, Linux, UNIX, and even an Apple computer without changing the program. It's for this reason that Java has become a popular programming language developers use to write a program that transforms an XML document. The program is referred to as a *transformer.*

A transformer reads a source file and transforms it into a results file (see Figure 7-3). The source file might be the true the DOM parser creates. The result might be an XML document that displays elements in a serial format (i.e., the standard XML format). The source can be any file or stream of characters. The result can also be any file or stream of data.

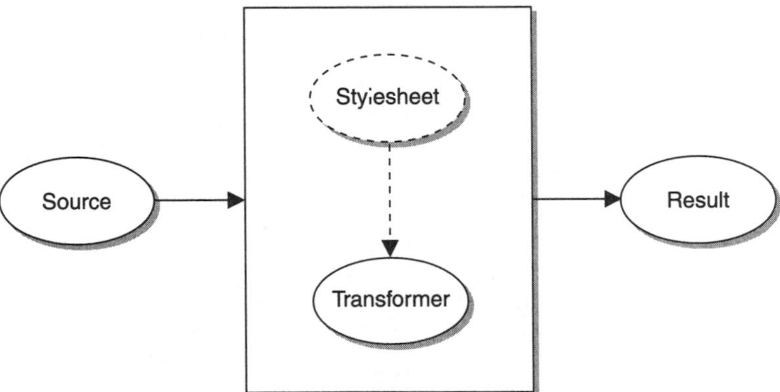

Figure 7-3 A transformer uses its own stylesheet to transform a source to a result.

For example, a transformer can read an XML document, transform it to HTML, and then send the HTML characters as a stream that's transmitted across the Internet to the browser that requested the document. The *Stream* is said to be a serial form of the source document. This is not quite right. The transformer can take a DOM, SAX, or Stream and the source and result. For example, you can start by creating a DOM object. The DOM object may be created from a Stream or created within memory (for example, building a new document). The DOM can then be transformed to a Stream. This uses the transformer to go from DOM to Stream, so the DOM is the source and the Stream is the result.

Java provides an API that enables you to apply stylesheets to the source document as the source is being transformed to the result. However, the stylesheet isn't referenced in the XML document as the XSLT is referenced. Instead, the stylesheet is referenced in the transformer and not the XML document.

This may appear strange at first, but it isn't when you consider that several web sites typically use the same XML document, and each site applies a different style to display the XML document. These web sites ignore references to the stylesheet if it's in the XML document because each site has its own transformer that contains its own stylesheet.

Looking Ahead

An XML document is transformed into a useful format by a parser. A parser is a program that adheres to one of two standards: the Simple API for XML (SAX) and Document Object Model (DOM). You use one of these standards to build parsers.

A SAX parser reads blocks of an XML document one at a time, and then transforms a block before reading the next one. This is why a SAX parser is ideal for reading very large XML documents. A SAX parser cannot create or modify an XML document.

A DOM parser reads the entire XML document and organizes the document into a tree structure in memory before transforming the XML document into another format. You must have sufficient memory available to hold the entire XML document; otherwise, you cannot use a DOM parser. A DOM parser can read, create, and modify an XML document.

Both the SAX parser and the DOM parser use the stylesheet that is referenced in the XML document. The stylesheet contains instructions on how to transform the XML document into another format. You must use the proper version of the SAX parser and the DOM parser that's suited for your computer. The transformer uses the stylesheet, and it overrides what's in the local document.

The Java transformer is a program written in the Java programming language that can run on any computer. It can read, create, and modify an XML document. However, the Java transformer uses its own stylesheet rather than the stylesheet that is referenced in the XML document. And unlike the SAX and DOM parsers, the same version of the Java transformer can be used on every Java-compatible computer.

Quiz

1. The SAX parser is able to transverse an XML document.
   a. True
   b. False
2. The SAX parser creates a node by using
   a. createElement()
   b. createTextNode()
   c. createComment()
   d. None of the above
3. The SAX parser reacts to a new element by using
   a. endElement()
   b. characters()
   c. startElement()
   d. startDocument()
4. Which of the following is represented as a node in the tree a DOM parser creates?
   a. CDATA sections
   b. Comments
   c. Elements
   d. All of the above
5. A Java transformer can use
   a. Its own stylesheet
   b. DTD

c. XSLT

d. All of the above

6. The same version of a DOM parser must be used on all computers.

   a. True

   b. False

7. A Stream is a series of characters that can be the results of transformation performed by a Java transformer.

   a. True

   b. False

8. A SAX parser

   a. Reads a block of an XML document at a time

   b. Organizes the XML document into a tree

   c. Enables you to correct the contents of an XML document

   d. None of the above

9. You should use a SAX parser if a DOM parser is unable to load the XML document into memory.

   a. True

   b. False

10. The appendChild() method links a node to the current node.

   a. True

   b. False

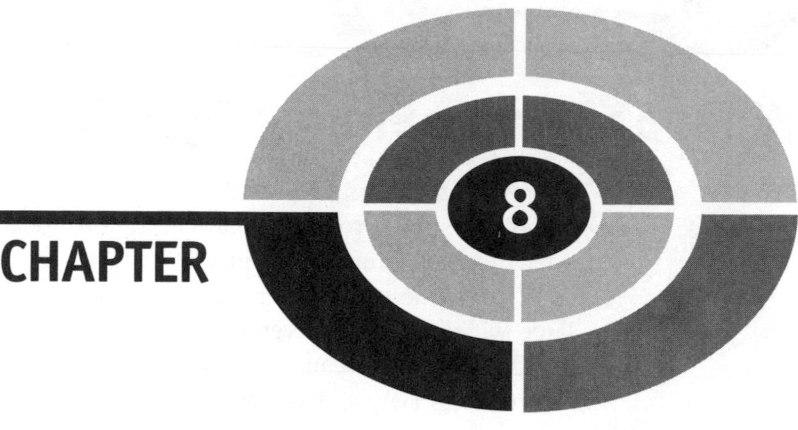

CHAPTER 8

Really Simple Syndication (RSS)

XML is more than theory. It's used in real-world applications to transfer information between different applications, eliminating the need for developers to write complex programs to access data from databases. In this chapter, we'll explore one of those real-world applications called Really Simple Syndication (RSS).

If you've ever wished there was a way to distribute your web content to the millions of web sites on the Internet, then you'll enjoy reading this chapter. RSS is an application of XML that you use to register your content with companies called *aggregators*. Aggregators are like a chain of supermarkets for web site content.

In this chapter, you'll learn how to create an RSS document that contains all the information an aggregator requires to offer your content to other web site operators.

What Is Really Simple Syndication (RSS)?

RSS is a method that uses XML to distribute a document published on a web site to other web sites, similar to how an article in your local newspaper is picked up by the news wire services and distributed to other media outlets.

Dave Winer came up with this idea back in 1997. Netscape adopted RSS two years later, which made their version of RSS the de facto standard. Winer updated RSS in 2003 after Netscape discontinued RSS development. Today there are several companies (www.newsisfree.com and www.syndic8.com) that offer a free aggregation service using RSS. The aggregator, similar to a news wire service, gathers documents from a variety of web sites and makes them available for publication by other web sites.

Here's how RSS works. First you format your document using RSS-defined XML tags and then post the document on your web site. Next, you register with an aggregator. Each day the aggregator polls registered web sites for RSS documents.

When polling a registered web site, the aggregator verifies the link and then displays information about the feed so clients can sort through topics and link to documents that interest them. RSS XML tags contain values that identify the document and parts of the document, which helps the client determine which parts to display on their web site.

For example, you might display a book review on your web site. The RSS XML tags enable you to identify the topic of your review and to identify its parts, such as the headline, subheadline, synopsis, and full review.

The client who wants to publish your review can decide to display only the headline; the headline and the synopsis; the headline, the subheadline, and the synopsis; or the complete review. The client links to your document rather than storing your document on its own web server.

Inside an RSS Document

Let's say that you wrote two articles: one titled "Risk Mitigation in IT Projects" and the other titled "Outsourcing Myths and Misconceptions." You want to make both available to other web sites by using the RSS feed. The *RSS feed* is the term developers call the process of distributing an RSS XML document.

Here's the RSS document that you need to prepare:

```
<?xml version="1.0" ?>
<rss version="2.0">
```

```
<!-- my first RSS document -->
   <channel>
      <title>Jim Keogh Home Page</title>
      <link>http://www.jimkeogh.com</link>
      <description>Jim Keogh Lecture Series</description>
      <item>
         <title>Risk Mitigation in IT Projects</title>
         <link>http://www.jimkeogh.com/riskmitigation/</link>
         <description>Seminar on limiting risks in
               large IT projects</description>
      </item>
      <item>
         <title>Outsourcing Myths and Misconceptions</title>
         <link>http://www.jimkeogh.com/outsourcing/</link>
         <description>Real world examples
            and issues with outsourcing</description>
      </item>
   </channel>
</rss>
```

The first thing you'll notice is that the RSS document doesn't contain the articles. Instead, it contains a description of each article and the link to the article. The client links to the article if they have an interest in publishing the article.

The first line of the RSS document is the XML declaration that identifies the XML version used in the document. Following this is the RSS declaration that identifies the version of RSS the document uses.

You can insert a comment anywhere in your RSS document by using the <!-- and --> symbols, which are the same as comments in HTML. This example contains one comment that identifies this as your first RSS document.

The rss element is the outermost tag of the RSS document and it contains the RSS elements that are used to describe the feed. In this example, the channel is the RSS element that's used to describe the feed.

The channel element has three child elements. These are

- **title** The title element defines the title of the channel. In this example, Jim Keogh Home Page is the title.
- **link** The link element identifies the hyperlink of the web site that's associated with this channel. It's important not to confuse this link with the link to an article. These are separate links.
- **description** The description element contains text that describes the channel, which is the web site www.jimkeogh.com.

Each channel can have one or more item elements. An item element defines an article that the RSS aggregator is distributing. Information defined in an item element appears on the RSS aggregator web site. There are two item elements in this example: the Risk Mitigation in IT Projects article and the Outsourcing Myths and Misconceptions article.

Each item element has three child elements. These are

- **title** The title element is the title of the item. Remember that the text you enter in the title element is the title that appears on the aggregator's web site.
- **link** The link element is the link to the article on your web site. Make sure that you provide the full path to the article; otherwise, the client won't be able to link to the article.
- **description** The description element provides a brief description for the article. The content of the description is very important because clients use it to determine if they'll select the article for publication. Some clients will simply display the title, link, and description on their web sites and then it's up to their web site visitors to decide whether or not to link to your article.

More About the channel Element

The channel element contains other child elements (we didn't use them in the previous example). However, it's useful to include some of these child elements in the RSS document because they provide the aggregator and, ultimately, the client with more information that describes the channel.

The category child element enables the aggregator to place your feed into a group of feeds within the same category. Clients are then able to visit the aggregator's web site and drill down into the category to see feeds that specialize in topics that interest them.

A channel category for our example might be

```
<category>Lecture Series</category>
```

The category element can also be used for item elements. This enables you to place your document within a category, making it easy for the client to find it. For example, good categories for our documents would be

```
<category>IT Projects</category>
<category>Outsourcing</category>
```

The copyright element is another useful element within the channel element. It displays notice that the copyright law protects the material referenced in the RSS document. Some aggregators display the copyright element so clients can determine if the channel's offerings are current.

Here's how to use the copyright element:

```
<copyright>2007 Jim Keogh, Inc.</copyright>
```

You can dress up your RSS document with an image such as a logo that some aggregators will display on their web sites when showing your offerings. You do this by using the image element within the channel element.

The image element requires you to include three child elements. These are

- **url** The url element contains the link to the image.
- **title** The title element specifies text that's displayed if the aggregator is unable to display the image. This is similar to the alt attribute in the HTML image tag.
- **link** The link element defines the link to the web site that's offering the channel.

Here's how to use the image element in your RSS document. The image is contained in the logo.gif file. The Lecture Series text is displayed in place of the image if the image cannot be displayed. The channel is provided by www.jimkeogh.com.

```
<?xml version="1.0" ?>
<rss version="2.0">
   <channel>
      ...
      <image>
         <url>http://www.jimkeogh.com/lectures/logo.gif</url>
         <title>Lecture Series</title>
         <link>http://www.jimkeogh.com</link>
      </image>
      ...
   </channel>
</rss>
```

You'll probably recall times when you Googled an expression and received links that are written in different languages. The same thing happens when aggregators list RSS documents. Some are written in English and others are written in other languages.

You can specify the language used to write your document by specifying the language element in the RSS document. The language element must specify the language code that conforms to the ISO 639 standards. Here's how you'd specify U.S. English:

```
<language>us-en</language>
```

Communicating with the Aggregator

You can use elements within the channel element to provide the aggregator with information about when the aggregator should update its copy of your RSS document. There are five elements that are frequently used in the RSS document: pubDate, skipDays, skipHours, ttl, and webMaster.

<pubDate>

The pubDate element is where you place the date that you last updated your RSS document. The aggregator might review the contents of this element before updating your RSS document on its web site.

The date must be in the data and time format specification of the RFC 822 as shown here:

```
<pubDate>Mon, 06 Mar 2006 12:00:00 GMT</pubDate>
```

<skipDays>

You use the skipDays element to tell the aggregator to skip updating your RSS document on certain days. For example, some developers don't update their RSS document on the weekends, so they place Saturday and Sunday in the skipDays element.

The skipDays element requires that you use at least one day child element. The day child element is where you place the name of the day that the aggregator doesn't have to update its copy of your RSS document. You can have up to seven day child elements in the skipDays element. Here's how you skip updating on the weekend:

```
<skipDays>
   <day>Saturday</day>
   <day>Sunday</day>
</skipDays>
```

<skipHours>

If you know that your last update of the RSS document is always at 5 p.m. and never before 9 a.m., then you can tell the aggregator to skip updating its copy of your RSS document after 5 p.m. and before 9 a.m. by using the skipHours child element.

The skipHours child element requires at least one hour child element and can have up to 24 hour child elements. Each hour child element must contain an integer that represents the hour you want the aggregator to skip the update. The hour child element uses the 24-hour clock where 0 is one o'clock in the morning and 23 is midnight.

Here's how to tell the aggregator to skip the updates after normal business hours:

```
<skipHours>
   <hour>0</hour>
   <hour>1</hour>
   <hour>2</hour>
   <hour>3</hour>
   <hour>4</hour>
   <hour>5</hour>
   <hour>6</hour>
   <hour>7</hour>
   <hour>17</hour>
   <hour>18</hour>
   <hour>19</hour>
   <hour>20</hour>
   <hour>21</hour>
   <hour>22</hour>
   <hour>23</hour>
</skipHours>
```

<ttl>

The ttl (time to live) element specifies the number of minutes that the RSS document has before the copy of the RSS document in cache is refreshed. The RSS document is placed in cache (memory) the first time it's loaded. During the session, the RSS document is displayed from cache when subsequent requests are made for the RSS document.

Retrieving the RSS document from cache rather than from the server provides a quick response; however, the contents of the copy of the RSS document in cache can easily be outdated. In order to avoid this problem you use the ttl element to set the number of minutes that the RSS document can remain in cache; after this expires, the RSS document must be refreshed from the server.

Let's say that your RSS documents almost always remains unchanged for two hours. Therefore, you can set the ttl element to 120 minutes. This means that the aggregator is asked to refresh its copy of the RSS document that's stored in cache every 120 minutes.

<webMaster>

It's important that the aggregator has a way to communicate directly to you should anything go wrong when it's accessing your RSS document or links that are embedded in the document. The best way to open the line of communication with the aggregator is to use the webMaster element.

The webMaster element is where you place the e-mail address of the person who responds to inquiries from the aggregator. Here's what you need to write:

```
<webMaster>jm@jimkeogh.com</webMaster>
```

More About the item Element

You'll recall from earlier in this chapter that the item element is used to identify XML documents in the RSS document that you have available for publication. The example of the RSS document we show in the "Inside an RSS Document" section contained the minimum information that you need to include in the item element. However, there are additional child elements that you can use to provide the aggregator with more information about the publication.

Here are the six most commonly used child elements for an item element.

<author>

You use the author element to provide the aggregator with the author's e-mail address. Some developers opt not to include this to prevent spammers from acquiring the e-mail address. Here's how you write the author element:

```
<author>jm@jimkeogh.com</author>
```

<comments>

Sometimes you'll want to provide the aggregator with additional information about an item that you don't want published on the aggregator's web site. Place this information in a document and then reference that document in the comments element, as we show here. The itemcomments is the document that contains the comments.

```
<comments>http://www.jimkeogh.com/itemcomments</comments>
```

<enclosure>

You use the enclosure element if you have a media file that you want to include with the item in the RSS document. For example, you might record a brief audio message

that encourages clients to publish your document. You can include that with the item by using the following enclosure element:

```
<enclosure url="http://www.jimkeogh.com/lecture1.mp3" length="6000"
type="audio/mpeg" />
```

You must include three attributes with the enclosure element:

- **url** The url is the link to the media file. In this example, lecture1.mp3 is the name of the media file.
- **length** The length attribute specifies the size of the media file in bytes. This example is 6000 bytes in length.
- **type** The type attribute states the type of media file. The media file in this example is an audio file using the mpeg format.

<guid>

You use the guid element to assign the item a unique value called the Globally Unique Identifier (GUID). You create the ID from a string, numeric value, URL, or any character that uniquely identifies the item. The aggregator can use this ID to determine if its copy of the RSS document has been updated.

Here's how to write the guid element:

```
<guid>http://www.jimkeogh.com/lecture1234</guid>
```

<pubDate>

The pubDate element is identical to the pubDate element used in the category element. The pubDate element here specifies the date that the item was published or updated. This follows the same description for the category element (see the "Communicating with the Aggregator" section).

<source>

You use the source element to identify a file used for the item a third party provides. This enables you to combine resources obtained from other web sites (with permission) into your RSS document.

Here's how to write the source element:

```
<source url="http://thirdpartycontent.com/content">Some other site</source>
```

Looking Ahead

Really Simple Syndication (RSS) is an application of XML that enables content providers to make their documents available to other web sites using an aggregator much like a local newspaper distributes their news stories to media outlets using a news wire service.

In order to distribute their content, the content provider creates an RSS document using XML. The RSS document provides the aggregator with general information regarding the content provider and with specific information about each item the content provider offers.

The rss element encloses child elements that describe the RSS document. Within the rss element is the channel element, which identifies the content provider and contains one or more item elements.

The item element describes a document that the content provider is publishing. This element includes the title of the document, the URL that contains the document, and a brief description of the item. The aggregator typically displays information in the item element on the aggregator's web site so clients can pick and choose the context they want published on their web sites.

You can enhance both the channel and the item elements by using one of a series of other child elements that, among other things, associates a channel with a specific category of other channels.

Once you've created the RSS document, it's registered with an aggregator. The aggregator then makes a copy of the RSS document and uses it to display the items on the aggregator web site in the hope that clients will want to use it on their own web sites.

The RSS document contains only references to documents and not the actual document. Clients who want to use the document on their web sites read the RSS document and then update their web sites with links contained in the RSS document.

Quiz

1. An aggregator is a web site that offers content to other web site operators.
   a. True
   b. False
2. What element do you use to display your logo on the aggregator's web site?
   a. logoElement
   b. imageElement

  c. image
  d. None of the above

3. The comment element is used to
   a. Display comments in the RSS document
   b. Display comments in the article document
   c. Tell the aggregator when to find a document that contains comments
   d. Contain test, which is hidden from the aggregator
4. The skipDays element is used to
   a. Tell the client that the documents are out of date
   b. Tell the aggregator days that you don't want the aggregator to update its copy of your RSS document
   c. Tell the aggregator you no longer want your documents distributed
   d. All of the above
5. What does the value 21 in the hour element tell the aggregator to do?
   a. Don't update for the next 21 hours
   b. Update only at 8 p.m.
   c. Don't update at 9 p.m.
   d. Don't update at 8 p.m.
6. Registering your RSS document with an aggregator guarantees a wide distribution of your documents.
   a. True
   b. False
7. You specify the language used to write your document by using the ISO 639 standard in the language element.
   a. True
   b. False
8. Which of the following is a GUID for an item?
   a. atdecb
   b. 45727
   c. 3rs3567dvg
   d. All of the above

9. The link element within the image element identifies the web site that's responsible for the image.
   a. True
   b. False
10. You use the enclosure element if you have a media file that you want to include with an item in the RSS document.
    a. True
    b. False

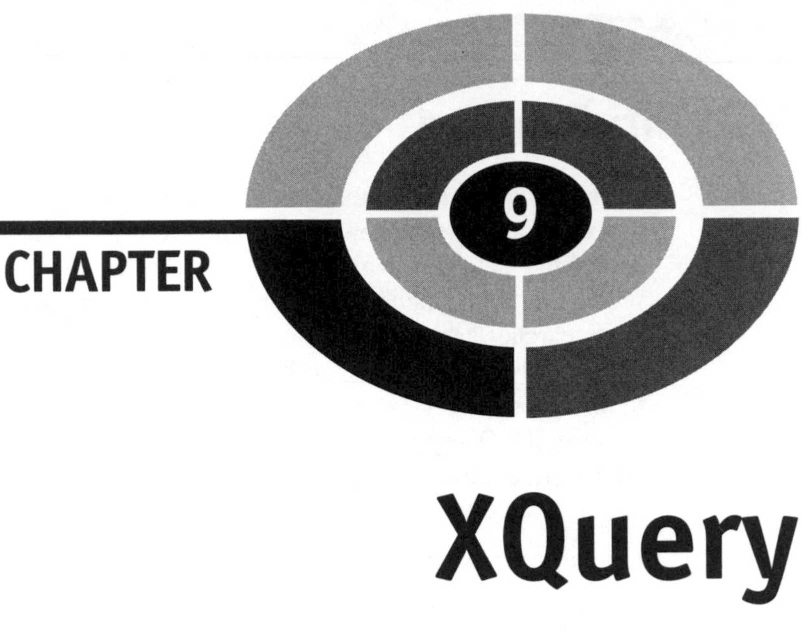

XQuery

A customer calls you asking a question about her order. You need to quickly access her order; however, all orders are stored in a very long XML document. It's too time-consuming to search through each line of the XML document. What do you do? You could panic and have an unhappy customer, or you can create an XQuery to electronically search for and display the customer's order.

Think of XQuery as your electronic assistant who knows where to find any information in an XML document as fast as your computer will allow. Your job is to use the proper expression to request the information. XQuery interprets your request and retrieves the information that you need from the XML document.

The way you use XQuery is similar to how you use SQL to access information from a relational database. The relational database is like an XML document—both contain lots of information, making it inefficient to search by hand.

In this chapter, you'll harness the power of XQuery by learning how to write expressions that enable you to tap into the vast treasure trove of information stored in an XML document.

Getting Started

There are a few things that you'll need to do before you write your first XQuery expression. XQuery is an extension of XPath; therefore, make sure that you read Chapter 6 before moving ahead with this chapter. You'll also need an XQuery processor. An XQuery processor is the software that's like an electronic assistant who searches an XML document for information you request. Skip this section if you already have installed an XQuery processor; otherwise, read on and learn how to install one.

Several XQuery processors are available. Some are freeware or open source, and others are commercial software products. Let's save a few dollars. Download the Saxon-B version 8, which is an open source XQuery processor, at:

```
http://saxon.sourceforge.net/
```

Saxon-B is a zip file. Download it to c:\saxon and then unzip the file. That's all you need to do to install Saxon-B.

Saxon-B is a Java program. Therefore, you'll also need to have a runtime version of Java installed on your computer. You'll find a free, downloadable copy at:

```
http://java.sun.com
```

Download the latest version of Java 2 Standard Edition (J2SE) and follow the installation instructions that come with the downloaded file. You don't need to know anything about Java to run Saxon-B with the examples we show in this chapter. Take note of where you install the Java runtime. You will need to know this to execute the samples.

Testing Saxon-B

Once you've installed the software, you'll need to make sure everything is working properly. To do this, create an XML document and an XQuery, and then use Saxon-B to retrieve information from the XML document.

Here's the XML document that you'll use to learn XQuery. Write this document using an editor and save it in the saxon directory as catalog.xml:

```
<?xml version="1.0"?>
<catalog>
   <cd upc="602498678299">
      <artist>U2</artist>
      <title>How to Dismantle an Atomic Bomb</title>
      <price>13.98</price>
      <label>Interscope Records</label>
      <date>2004-11-23</date>
```

```
   </cd>
   <cd upc="75679244222">
      <artist>Led Zeppelin</artist>
      <title>Physical Graffiti</title>
      <price>22.99</price>
      <label>Atlantic</label>
      <date>1994-08-16</date>
   </cd>
   <cd upc="75678367229">
      <artist>Rush</artist>
      <title>Rush in Rio</title>
      <price>13.98</price>
      <label>Atlantic</label>
      <date>2003-10-21</date>
   </cd>
   <cd upc="74646938720">
      <artist>Billy Joel</artist>
      <title>Songs in the Attic</title>
      <price>10.99</price>
      <label>Sony</label>
      <date>1998-10-20</date>
   </cd>
   <cd upc="75678263927">
      <artist>Led Zeppelin</artist>
      <title>Houses of the Holy</title>
      <price>10.98</price>
      <label>Atlantic</label>
      <date>1994-07-19</date>
   </cd>
   <cd upc="8811160227">
      <artist>Jimi Hendrix</artist>
      <title>Are You Experienced?</title>
      <price>12.99</price>
      <label>Experience Hendrix</label>
      <date>1997-04-22</date>
   </cd>
   <cd upc="74640890529">
      <artist>Bob Dylan</artist>
      <title>The Times They Are A-Changin'</title>
      <price>9.99</price>
      <label>Sony</label>
      <date>1990-10-25</date>
   </cd>
</catalog>
```

Next, you'll need to create the XQuery. Type the following XQuery into your editor and save it in the saxon directory in a file called catalog.xq. This XQuery retrieves and displays a list of titles contained in the XML document. Although the XQuery probably looks strange to you, you'll understand each line of the XQuery by the time you finish reading this chapter.

```
<html>
<body>
   List of titles in this catalog:
   <br/>
   <ul>
   {
      for $x in doc("catalog.xml")/catalog/cd/title
         order by $x
         return <li>{data($x)}</li>
   }
   </ul>
</body>
</html>
```

The final step to test Saxon-B is to execute the XQuery. Here's what you need to do:

1. Open a Command Prompt window if you're using a Windows computer.
2. Make saxon the current directory.
3. Type the following command:

   ```
   c:\Saxon> c:\jdk15\bin\java -cp saxon8.jar net.sf.saxon.Query -t catalog
   .xq > output.html
   ```

4. Press ENTER.

This command probably looks like a bunch of gibberish. It isn't. The first part (c:\jdk15\bin\java) specifies the path to Java and runs Java. The second part (-cp saxon8.jar net.sf.saxon.Query) tells Java to extract the Query portion of the saxon8 .jar file, which is the file that contains Saxon-B. The third part (-t catalog.xq) of the command identifies the XQuery file, which is catalog.xq. The last part (> output .html) redirects the result of running the XQuery to the file called output.html.

Tip *The jdk15 portion of the first part of the command is the directory where Java is installed on our computer. You probably installed Java in a different directory so you'll need to replace jdk15 with the name of the directory on your computer where you installed Java.*

You can use this same command to run all the examples in this chapter; however, for each example you'll need to change the name of the query from catalog.xq to the name we give to the query.

Nothing much happens when you run Saxon-B—at least nothing you can see on the screen. Open the output.html in an editor and you'll see the result of your XQuery. It should look like this:

```
<html>
   <body>
      List of titles in this catalog:<br><ul>
         <li>Are You Experienced?</li>
         <li>Houses of the Holy</li>
         <li>How to Dismantle an Atomic Bomb</li>
         <li>Physical Graffiti</li>
         <li>Rush in Rio</li>
         <li>Songs in the Attic</li>
         <li>The Times They Are A-Changin'</li>
      </ul>
   </body>
</html>
```

Figure 9-1 shows the result of your XQuery when it's displayed by a browser.

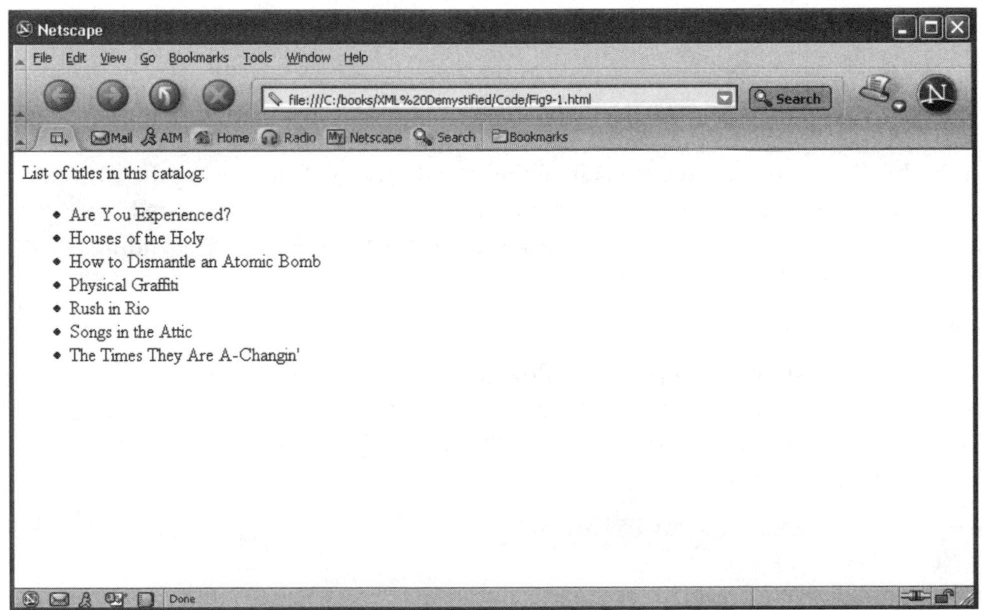

Figure 9-1 Your browser displays the result of your XQuery request.

How XQuery Works

An XQuery must contain a conditional expression that specifies the search criteria. A conditional expression is either true or false. For example, /catalog/cd/title = 'XML Demystified' is a conditional expression. Saxon-B looks at the next title tag in the XML document and determines if the text of the title tag is 'XML Demystified'. If so, then the conditional expression is true; otherwise, the conditional expression is false.

A conditional expression is used within a FLWOR expression. FLWOR sounds like more gibberish, but it's really an acronym for for, let, where, order by, and return clauses. A clause is a component of an XQuery.

For, Let, and Order By Clauses

You use the for and let clauses to assign values to variables within the XQuery. A variable is a placeholder for a value such as $x. Look at the catalog.xq file and you'll notice the following for clause. For each title tag in the catalog XML file, Saxon-B assigns the text of the current title XML tag to the $x variable and then sorts the titles.

```
for $x in doc("catalog.xml")/catalog/cd/title
```

Look at the code that follows the for clause and you'll see that variable $x is used by the order by clause. The text of the title replaces the $x variable when Saxon-B runs the XQuery before processing the order by clause.

The order by clause places the value of $x in sorted order. In this example, the order by clause sorts all the titles in alphabetical order before storing the titles into the output.html file. Titles within the XML document remain unchanged.

You can specify the direction of the sort by using ascending or descending, as we show here. The default direction is ascending.

```
order by $x descending
```

The let clause, not used in the catalog.xq example, assigns a value to a variable. Suppose you want to assign the title 'XML Demystified' to variable $x. Here's how you write the let clause to do this. You can then use $x in place of 'XML Demystified' throughout the XQuery.

```
let $x := 'XML Demystified'
```

The Where and Return Clauses

You use the where clause to specify a filter criterion using a conditional expression. Let's say that you want to see titles by Jimi Hendrix. You can use the where clause

to tell Saxon-B to compare the text of the artist tag to Jimi Hendrix. If there is a match, then the text of the title tag is assigned the variable $x, which is then used by the order by clause to sort all titles by Jimi Hendrix. This is illustrated in the following segment of the XQuery.

```
for $x in doc("catalog.xml")/catalog/cd/title
   where doc("catalog.xml")/catalog/cd/artist = 'Jimi Hendrix'
order by $x
```

The return clause identifies information that Saxon-B returns to the output.html file. It can return literal characters, the content of tags in an XML document, and the value of variables used within the XQuery.

The catalog.xq XQuery uses the return clause to return HTML characters and the value of the $x. The HTML characters format the data for the browser. The data($x) function is called to return the text associated with $x. Remember $x is the title element that includes the markup tag and any child nodes. The data() function extracts the text from between the tags, for example:

```
$x equals:    <title>How to Dismantle an Atomic Bomb</title>
data($x) equals:  How to Dismantle an Atomic Bomb
```

A function is a task that Saxon-B performs. You call the function by name anytime you want the task to be performed in your XQuery. This is referred to as a function call and must be contained with French braces ({ }). This example calls the data() function, which extracts the text from the argument:

```
return <li>{data($x)}</li>
```

A Walkthrough of an XQuery

Let's take a closer look at the catalog.xq now that you have an understanding of how clauses work. The catalog.xq is basically an HTML document that has XQuery clauses embedded in it. (Our example is converting to HTML, but it can be to any language you like.)

You probably recognized the first part of the XQuery because it's HTML. The <body> tag contains text that's displayed on the screen followed by an unordered list.

```
<html>
<body>
   List of titles in this catalog:
   <br/>
   <ul>
```

Next is the meat of the XQuery. This is where you tell Saxon-B the information that you want returned from the XML document. It begins with an open French brace ({) and ends with a closed French brace (}).

```
{
   for $x in doc("catalog.xml")/catalog/cd/title
   order by $x
   return <li>{data($x)}</li>
}
```

The first line within the French brace is the for clause, which you learned about previously in this chapter. The for clause tells Saxon-B to look for something within the XML document. In this case the something is the title tag.

You must tell Saxon-B to retrieve the XML document and then specify all the parent tags, if any, of the tag that you want returned. Retrieving the XML document is a task. You have Saxon-B do this by calling the doc() function and passing it the name of the XML document. The parent tags are catalog and cd.

Each time Saxon-B encounters the title tag in the XML document it assigns the title tag to variable $x. Once the end of the XML document is reached, Saxon-B sorts titles contained in variable $x.

The return clause is then called to return all the titles to the output.html file. Notice that the <li> HTML tag is part of the return value, which causes titles to be displayed on a bulleted list.

The last part of the XQuery is also familiar because it contains the closing HTML tags for the tags opened in the first part of the XQuery.

```
   </ul>
</body>
</html>
```

Constructors

Information contained in an XML document is stored as a series of characters called a string. This isn't a problem unless you want to use the information in a calculation; then you need to convert the character to a type of information that can be calculated. There are several types of data, which are referred to as data types. You're familiar with most of them. These are numbers, decimals, dates, and Boolean. Boolean is true or false. And, of course, there is a string.

Let's say that you want to calculate the sales tax for a CD. The price of the CD is $19.95 and is in the XML document. However, $19.95 is a string and not a

number. Therefore, you must convert $19.95 from a string to a decimal. A decimal contains both a whole number and a decimal number.

You can convert information contained in an XML document to another data type by using a constructor. A constructor tries to convert the content of an XML tag to a data type. If it fails, then it returns an error. Table 9-1 contains a list of constructors. You use them within the XQuery to convert information from the XML document into a different data type so it can be used in a calculation.

A constructor requires you to pass it the name of the tag. The constructor then returns the converted value. Typically you'll assign the converted value to a variable and then use the variable in a calculation.

Here's how to convert the CD price to a decimal value. The xs:decimal() is the constructor. The doc() function retrieves the catalog.xml document that contains the price. /catalog/cd/price are parent/child tags that identify the tag whose text is being converted to a decimal. The converted value is assigned to the $price variable:

```
let $price := xs:decimal(doc("catalog.xml")/catalog/cd /price)
```

Constructors are frequently used in the conditional statements in a where clause to compare the search criteria to the value of the XML tag. Let's say that you want to extract the title and price of all the CDs that are less than $11.00 with a release date greater than 1993-10-31.

In order to do this, you need to convert the text of the price tag to a decimal and the text of the date tag to a date data type. Once they're converted, you can write a conditional statement that compares these values against the search criteria.

Constructor	Description
xs:decimal	Constructs a decimal value from a string. The string must be a number.
xs:date	Constructs a date value from a string. The string must conform to the pattern YYYY-MM-DD; for example, 2006-10-31.
xs:double	Constructs a double precision floating point number from a string.
xs:float	Constructs a floating point number from a string.
xs:hexBinary	Constructs a hex binary value from a string.
xs:int	Constructs an integer from a string.
xs:time	Constructs a time.

Table 9-1 Constructors Used to Convert XML Strings

Let's walk through the next example and see how this works. The for clause opens the catalog XML document and assigns the /catalog/cd tags to the $cd variable. You then combine the $cd variable with the /price tag and the /date tag in the constructors. You do this to make the code easier to read. You could have passed the complete parent/child tags to the constructor such as we did in the example we show earlier in this section.

You use the xs:decimal() constructor and the xs:date() constructor to convert the price and the date to its respective data type and assign the converted value to variables. You then use variables in the conditional expression of the where clause. The value of the $price variable is compared to 11.00 and the value of the $date variable is compared to 1993-10-31. Notice that 1993-10-31 must also be converted to a date because "1993-10-31" is a string just like the date in the XML document. You use the less than operator (<) to determine if the value of the price variable is less than 11.00; and use the greater than operator (>) to determine if the value of the date variable is greater than 1993-10-31. Both conditions must be true for the conditional statement to be true, and for information about the CD to be returned by the XQuery.

```
<html>
<body>
   List of titles in this catalog:<br/>
   <ul>
   {
      for $cd in doc("catalog.xml")/catalog/cd
        let $price := xs:decimal($cd/price)
        let $date := xs:date($cd/date)
        where $price < 11.00 and $date > xs:date("1993-10-31")
      order by $date
      return <li>{data($cd/title)} - ${$price} - {$date}</li>
  }
   </ul>
</body>
</html>
```

Here's the result of this XQuery:

```
<html>
   <body>
      List of titles in this catalog:<br><ul>
         <li>Houses of the Holy - $10.98 - 1994-07-19</li>
         <li>Songs in the Attic - $10.99 - 1998-10-20</li>
      </ul>
   </body>
</html>
```

Figure 9-2 shows the result of the XQuery when it's displayed by a browser.

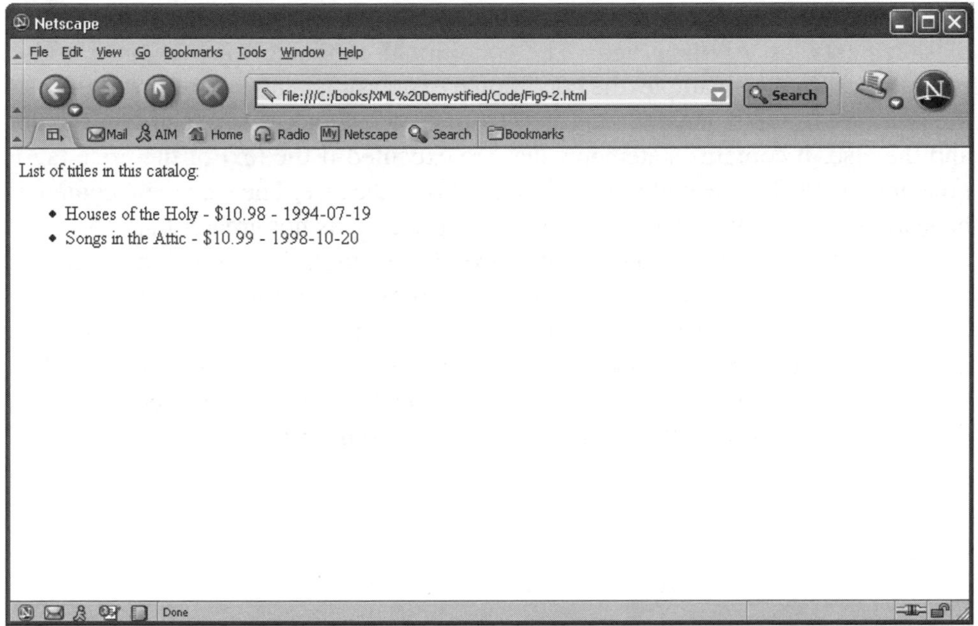

Figure 9-2 The XQuery result your browser displays.

Conditional Statements

A conditional statement specifies the search criteria for an XQuery. It simply tells Saxon-B to retrieve specific information from an XML document only if the information adheres to the conditional expression contained in the conditional statement.

A conditional expression contains operators and operands that resolve to either true or false. Operators include less than (<), greater than (>), equals (=), less than or equal to (<=), greater than or equal to (>=), and not equal to (!=). An operand is a value evaluated by an operator in a conditional expression. In this case, it's the name of the XML tag that contains the information that you want Saxon-B to compare to the search criteria—and the value of the search criteria is an operand as well.

A conditional statement is used in a for clause, which we explained earlier in the section "For, Let, and Order By Clauses". It's also used in an if…then…else statement. An if…then…else statement basically tells Saxon-B, "If the conditional expression is true, then execute these statements, else execute these other statements if the conditional expression is false."

The if…then…else statement contains a conditional expression and two blocks of statements, as we show here. The conditional expression is contained within parentheses. In this example, the conditional expression is testing where the text of the price XML tag is greater than 15. The first code block is between the if…then and the else. It contains statements that are executed if the text of the price tag is greater than 15. The second block of code follows the else. The statement contained beneath the else is executed if the text of the price tag is not greater than 15.

Notice that we use the round-half-to-even() function. This function rounds the calculated value. So 1.5 becomes 2 and 2.5 becomes 2. It rounds to the nearest even number. The round-half-to-even() function has two parameters. The first parameter is the value that's being rounded. In this case, we used a calculation. The result of the calculation is rounded. The second parameter is the number of decimal places that we want to show. In this example, we show two decimal places.

```
if($price > 15) then
   round-half-to-even($price * 0.8, 2)
else
   round-half-to-even($price * 0.9, 2)
```

Another form for an if…then…else statement is the if…then…else if…else statement. The if…then…else if…else statement is very similar to the if…then… else statement except that it contains two conditional statements.

The first conditional statement is the same as the one we show in the previous example. The second conditional statement is in the else if portion of the statement. This tells Saxon-B that if the first conditional statement is false, then test the second conditional statement. If the second conditional statement is true, then execute the statements between the else if and else. If the second conditional statement is false, then execute the statements that follow the else.

There are three code blocks in an if…then…else if…else statement, as we show here. The first code block is between the if…then and else if. The second code block is between the else if and else. And the third code block is after the else.

```
if($price > 15) then
   round-half-to-even($price * 0.8, 2)
else if($price > 11) then
   round-half-to-even($price * 0.9, 2)
else
   "No discount"
```

Suppose you want to extract the CD artist and title and then determine if a discount should be applied to the price. If the price is more than $15.00, then calculate a 20-percent discount. If the price is greater than $11.00 and less then or equal to $15.00, then calculate a 10-percent discount. There's no discount if the price is less than or equal to $11.00.

Here is the XQuery that you'll need to write to extract this information and perform these calculations. You'll notice that this is basically the same XQuery that you used throughout this chapter. However, we inserted an if…then…else if…else statement in the return clause of the XQuery. This conditional statement returns either the discounted price or the price itself if the price is less than or equal to $11.00. It also controls the format for decimal values.

```
<html>
<body>
   List of titles in this catalog:<br/>
   <table border="1">
      <tr>
         <td>Artist</td>
         <td>Title</td>
         <td>List Price</td>
         <td>Sale Price</td>
     </tr>
     {
        for $cd in doc("catalog.xml")/catalog/cd
           let $price := xs:decimal($cd/price)
           order by $cd/artist
        return
           <tr>
              <td>{data($cd/artist)}</td>
              <td>{data($cd/title)}</td>
              <td>{$price}</td>
              <td>
                {
                 if($price > 15) then
                    round-half-to-even($price * 0.8, 2)
                 else if($price > 11) then
                    round-half-to-even($price * 0.9, 2)
                 else
                    "No discount"
               }
             </td>
           </tr>
     }
   </table>
</body>
</html>
```

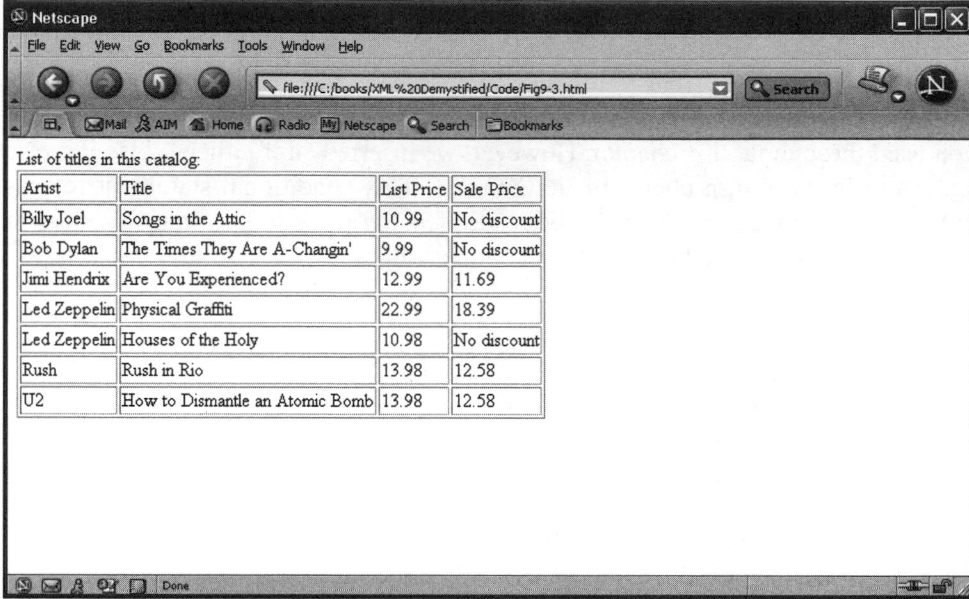

Figure 9-3 Here's the result of the XQuery when it's displayed in a browser.

Here's what the XQuery writes to the output.html file, and Figure 9-3 shows the result when it's displayed in a browser.

```
<html>
   <body>
      List of titles in this catalog:<br><table border="1">
         <tr>
            <td>Artist</td>
            <td>Title</td>
            <td>List Price</td>
            <td>Sale Price</td>
         </tr>
         <tr>
            <td>Billy Joel</td>
            <td>Songs in the Attic</td>
            <td>10.99</td>
            <td>No discount</td>
         </tr>
```

```
            <tr>
               <td>Bob Dylan</td>
               <td>The Times They Are A-Changin'</td>
               <td>9.99</td>
               <td>No discount</td>
            </tr>
            <tr>
               <td>Jimi Hendrix</td>
               <td>Are You Experienced?</td>
               <td>12.99</td>
               <td>11.69</td>
            </tr>
            <tr>
               <td>Led Zeppelin</td>
               <td>Physical Graffiti</td>
               <td>22.99</td>
               <td>18.39</td>
            </tr>
            <tr>
               <td>Led Zeppelin</td>
               <td>Houses of the Holy</td>
               <td>10.98</td>
               <td>No discount</td>
            </tr>
            <tr>
               <td>Rush</td>
               <td>Rush in Rio</td>
               <td>13.98</td>
               <td>12.58</td>
            </tr>
            <tr>
               <td>U2</td>
               <td>How to Dismantle an Atomic Bomb</td>
               <td>13.98</td>
               <td>12.58</td>
            </tr>
         </table>
      </body>
   </html>
```

Retrieving the Value of an Attribute

Not all of the information is contained in the text of an XML tag. Sometimes information is assigned to an attribute of a tag, such as the UPC code in the CD tag that we show here:

```
<cd upc="75679244222">
```

You can use an XQuery to extract the value of an attribute by calling the data() function and specifying the @ symbol in front of the attribute name. Let's say that the UPC code is an attribute of the cd element and the cd element is the child of the catalog element. You then access the UPC code by using the following call to the data() function. You've seen something like this used previously in this chapter when you learned about how to use the data() function. The only new feature is the @ symbol, which you use to tell Saxon-B to use the value of the attribute rather than the text of the element.

```
{data(doc("catalog.xml")/catalog/cd/@upc)}
```

Here's the XQuery that accesses the value of the upc attribute. This is basically the same XQuery that you learned about previously in this chapter, except that you pass the @upc to the data() function.

```
<html>
<body>
   List of titles in this catalog:<br/>
   <table border="1">
      <tr>
         <td>UPC</td>
         <td>Artist</td>
         <td>Title</td>
      </tr>
      {
         for $cd in doc("catalog.xml")/catalog/cd
            order by $cd/artist
         return
         <tr>
            <td>{data($cd/@upc)}</td>
            <td>{data($cd/artist)}</td>
            <td>{data($cd/title)}</td>
         </tr>
      }
```

```
   </table>
</body>
</html>
```

Here's what the XQuery writes to the output.html file.

```
<html>
   <body>
      List of titles in this catalog:<br><table border="1">
      <tr>
         <td>UPC</td>
         <td>Artist</td>
         <td>Title</td>
      </tr>
      <tr>
         <td>74646938720</td>
         <td>Billy Joel</td>
         <td>Songs in the Attic</td>
      </tr>
      <tr>
         <td>74640890529</td>
         <td>Bob Dylan</td>
         <td>The Times They Are A-Changin'</td>
      </tr>
      <tr>
         <td>8811160227</td>
         <td>Jimi Hendrix</td>
         <td>Are You Experienced?</td>
      </tr>
      <tr>
         <td>75679244222</td>
         <td>Led Zeppelin</td>
         <td>Physical Graffiti</td>
      </tr>
      <tr>
         <td>75678263927</td>
         <td>Led Zeppelin</td>
         <td>Houses of the Holy</td>
      </tr>
      <tr>
         <td>75678367229</td>
         <td>Rush</td>
         <td>Rush in Rio</td>
```

```
        </tr>
        <tr>
            <td>602498678299</td>
            <td>U2</td>
            <td>How to Dismantle an Atomic Bomb</td>
        </tr>
    </table>
</body>
</html>
```

Here's what the XQuery writes to the output.html file, and Figure 9-4 shows the result when it's displayed in a browser.

Retrieving the Value of an Attribute and the Attribute Name

When you use the @ symbol followed by the attribute name without calling the data() function, an XQuery can return the name of the attribute, along with its value, as we illustrate here:

```
{$cd/@upc}
```

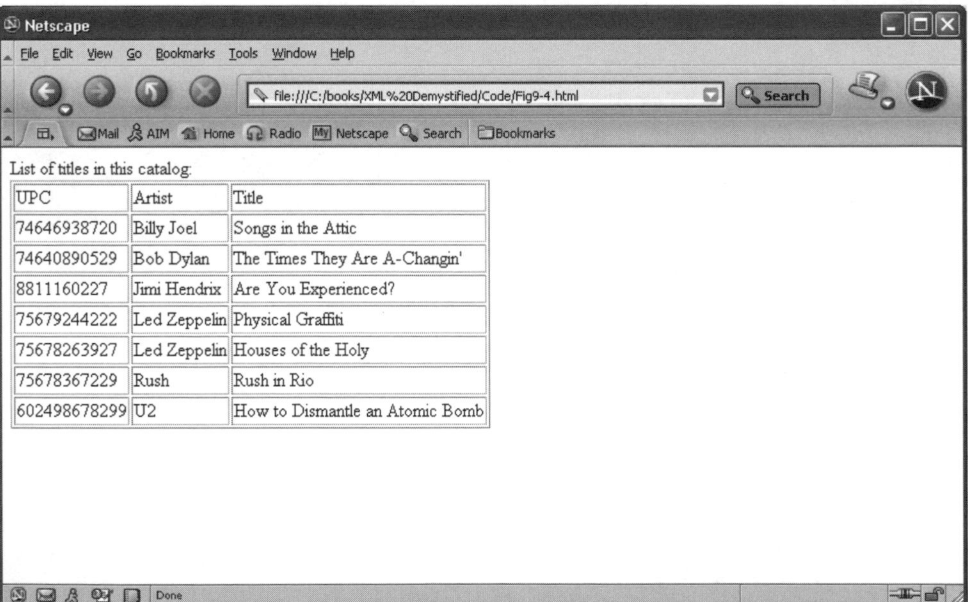

UPC	Artist	Title
74646938720	Billy Joel	Songs in the Attic
74640890529	Bob Dylan	The Times They Are A-Changin'
8811160227	Jimi Hendrix	Are You Experienced?
75679244222	Led Zeppelin	Physical Graffiti
75678263927	Led Zeppelin	Houses of the Holy
75678367229	Rush	Rush in Rio
602498678299	U2	How to Dismantle an Atomic Bomb

Figure 9-4 Here's how the UPC attribute appears when the output.html file is displayed in a browser.

Let's modify the previous XQuery to display both the UPC attribute name and its value. Here's the revised XQuery:

```
<html>
<body>
   List of titles in this catalog:<br/>
   <table border="1">
      <tr>
         <td>UPC</td>
         <td>Artist</td>
         <td>Title</td>
      </tr>
     {
        for $cd in doc("catalog.xml")/catalog/cd
           order by $cd/artist
        return
        <tr>
           <td>{$cd/@upc}</td>
           <td>{data($cd/artist)}</td>
           <td>{data($cd/title)}</td>
       </tr>
     }
   </table>
</body>
</html>
```

Here's the new output.html file. Notice that the attribute appears just as it does in the XML document. It has the attribute name, equal sign, and the value. Saxon-B is smart enough to replace the " that's in the XML document in double quotations.

```
<html>
   <body>
      List of titles in this catalog:<br><table border="1">
         <tr>
            <td>UPC</td>
            <td>Artist</td>
            <td>Title</td>
         </tr>
         <tr>
            <td upc="74646938720"></td>
            <td>Billy Joel</td>
            <td>Songs in the Attic</td>
         </tr>
         <tr>
```

```
            <td upc="74640890529"></td>
            <td>Bob Dylan</td>
            <td>The Times They Are A-Changin'</td>
         </tr>
         <tr>
            <td upc="8811160227"></td>
            <td>Jimi Hendrix</td>
            <td>Are You Experienced?</td>
         </tr>
         <tr>
            <td upc="75679244222"></td>
            <td>Led Zeppelin</td>
            <td>Physical Graffiti</td>
         </tr>
         <tr>
            <td upc="75678263927"></td>
            <td>Led Zeppelin</td>
            <td>Houses of the Holy</td>
         </tr>
         <tr>
            <td upc="75678367229"></td>
            <td>Rush</td>
            <td>Rush in Rio</td>
         </tr>
         <tr>
            <td upc="602498678299"></td>
            <td>U2</td>
            <td>How to Dismantle an Atomic Bomb</td>
         </tr>
      </table>
   </body>
</html>
```

CAUTION *Don't place text or any node before the attribute because it will cause an error. For example, the following statement confuses Saxon-B because the attribute is in the wrong location. Attributes are assigned first and then followed by the text of the element.*

```
<td> some other data {$cd/@upc}</td>
```

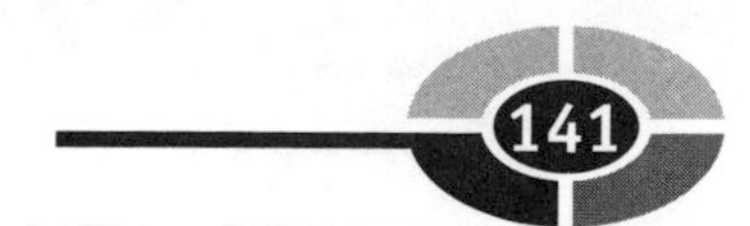

Functions

You already learned that a function is a task that Saxon-B already knows how to perform; all you need to do is to call the function in your XQuery whenever you want Saxon-B to perform that task.

Table 9-2 contains commonly used XQuery functions. You can find a complete list of functions at www.w3.org/2005/02/xpath-functions.

In addition to calling built-in functions, you can also define your own functions that can be called the same way a built-in function is called. Here's what you need to do. First create the function by writing a *function declaration statement*.

Function	Description	Example
upper-case()	Converts the argument to uppercase letters.	upper-case("Led Zeppelin") returns: "LED ZEPPELIN"
lower-case()	Converts the argument to lowercase letters.	lower-case("Led Zeppelin") returns: "led zeppelin"
substring()	Returns a substring.	substring("Led Zeppelin",1, 6) returns: "Led Ze"
string()	Returns the string representation of the argument.	string(645) returns: "645" as a string.
concat()	Returns the concatenation of two strings.	concat("XQu", "ery") returns: "XQuery"
string-join()	Returns a concatenation of the arguments separated by the specified separator. The first argument is a list of strings and the second argument is the separator. You may find this particularly useful for displaying names.	string-join(("Mary", "Ellen", "Smith"), " ") returns: "Mary Ellen Smith"
string-length()	Returns the length of the string. If the argument is a node, then it returns the length of the string data for that node.	string-length("Led Zeppelin") returns: 12

Table 9-2 Commonly Used Built-In XQuery Functions

The function declaration statement must have a prefix, a function name, a parameter list, and a return value. In addition, a function declaration statement must also define a code block that contains statements that are executed when the function is called from within an XQuery.

Here's the structure of a function declaration statement:

```
declare function prefix:function_name($parameter as datatype, ...)
   as returntype
{
     ... code for the function goes here...
};
```

Let's declare a function. You'll call it convertdate and it will convert the date format 2006-10-04 to October 4, 2006. The prefix will be called local. The parameter is the date that will be converted and the return value is the converted date.

Here's the function declaration. Notice that the parameter is placed within parentheses. You'll need to give the parameter a name and specify its data type. The name is always prefaced with a $ symbol. You'll also need to specify the data type of the value returned by the function. The return type in this example is a string.

The code block is defined with open and closed French braces ({ }). This is where you place statements that execute each time the function is called. The function begins by assigning all the months to an array called $month. An array is a variable that can have many values. Next, the month-from-date() function is called to extract the month of the date and assign it to the $month variable. The day-from-date() function and year-from-date() function are passed to the concat() function in the return clause to return the reformatted date.

The function declaration statement must appear at the top of the XQuery, as we show in the following example. Think of this as defining the function before you call the function within the XQuery. The function is called later in the XQuery {local:convertdate(xs:date($cd/date))}.

```
declare function local:convertdate($date as xs:date) as xs:string
{
   let $months := ("January","February","March","April","May",
         "June","July","August","September","October","November","December")
   let $month := $months[month-from-date($date)]
   return
   concat($month, " ", string(day-from-date($date)), ", ",
         string(year-from-date($date)))
};
<html>
<body>
```

```
    List of titles in this catalog:<br/>
    <table border="1">
        <tr>
          <td>UPC</td>
          <td>Artist</td>
          <td>Title</td>
          <td>Date</td>
       </tr>
    {
      for $cd in doc("catalog.xml")/catalog/cd
         order by $cd/artist
      return
      <tr>
         <td>{data($cd/@upc)}</td>
         <td>{data($cd/artist)}</td>
         <td>{data($cd/title)}</td>
         <td>{local:convertdate(xs:date($cd/date))}</td>
      </tr>
   }
   </table>
</body>
</html>
```

Here's the output.html file that the XQuery produces:

```
<html>
<body>
     List of titles in this catalog:<br><table border="1">
        <tr>
           <td>UPC</td>
           <td>Artist</td>
           <td>Title</td>
           <td>Date</td>
        </tr>
        <tr>
           <td>74646938720</td>
           <td>Billy Joel</td>
           <td>Songs in the Attic</td>
           <td>October 20, 1998</td>
        </tr>
        <tr>
           <td>74640890529</td>
           <td>Bob Dylan</td>
           <td>The Times They Are A-Changin'</td>
           <td>October 25, 1990</td>
```

```
            </tr>
            <tr>
               <td>8811160227</td>
               <td>Jimi Hendrix</td>
               <td>Are You Experienced?</td>
               <td>April 22, 1997</td>
            </tr>
            <tr>
               <td>75679244222</td>
               <td>Led Zeppelin</td>
               <td>Physical Graffiti</td>
               <td>August 16, 1994</td>
            </tr>
            <tr>
               <td>75678263927</td>
               <td>Led Zeppelin</td>
               <td>Houses of the Holy</td>
               <td>July 19, 1994</td>
            </tr>
            <tr>
               <td>75678367229</td>
               <td>Rush</td>
               <td>Rush in Rio</td>
               <td>October 21, 2003</td>
            </tr>
            <tr>
               <td>602498678299</td>
               <td>U2</td>
               <td>How to Dismantle an Atomic Bomb</td>
               <td>November 23, 2004</td>
            </tr>
         </table>
</body>
</html>
```

Here's how the output.html file appears when displayed in a browser (see Figure 9-5).

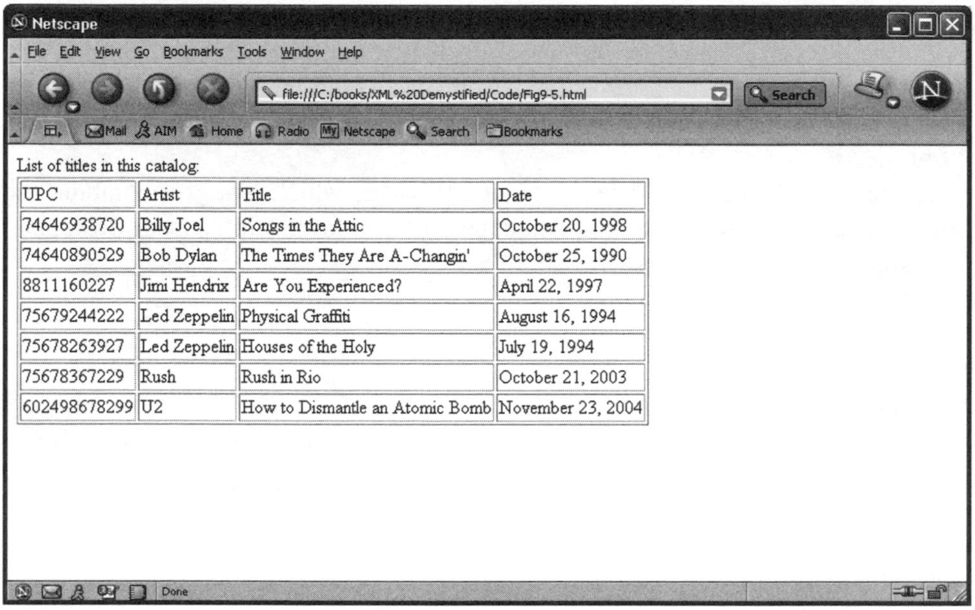

List of titles in this catalog:

UPC	Artist	Title	Date
74646938720	Billy Joel	Songs in the Attic	October 20, 1998
74640890529	Bob Dylan	The Times They Are A-Changin'	October 25, 1990
8811160227	Jimi Hendrix	Are You Experienced?	April 22, 1997
75679244222	Led Zeppelin	Physical Graffiti	August 16, 1994
75678263927	Led Zeppelin	Houses of the Holy	July 19, 1994
75678367229	Rush	Rush in Rio	October 21, 2003
602498678299	U2	How to Dismantle an Atomic Bomb	November 23, 2004

Figure 9-5 Here's how the output.html file is displayed in a browser.

Looking Ahead

XQuery is used to query information contained in an XML document. The XQuery is processed by the XQuery processor. Some of these processors are freeware or open source and others are commercial software products.

An XQuery is typed into an editor and saved to a file that contains the .xq file extension. The XQuery file is then passed to the XQuery processor as a command line argument. The result of the XQuery is contained in the output.html file, which you can open in your browser.

An XQuery contains conditional expressions that define search criteria. A conditional expression can be either true or false. Portions of the XML document that meet the search criteria are copied to the output.html file.

The for and let clauses are used to assign values to variables within the XQuery. The order by clause is used to sort the results in ascending or descending order. The where clause specifies a filter criteria using the conditional expression and the return clause identifies information that the XQuery processor returns to the output .html file.

In the next chapter you'll learn about MSXML, which lets you combine the power of XML and programming languages such as JavaScript, Visual Basic, and C++ when using Microsoft's XML Core Services.

Quiz

1. Saxon-B is the only software that can process an XQuery.
   a. True
   b. False
2. What kind of clause is used to specify the filter criteria?
   a. SQL clause
   b. Declarative clause
   c. where clause
   d. None of the above
3. $x is an
   a. Element
   b. Attribute
   c. XQuery
   d. Variable
4. Order by
   a. Places all elements in the XML document in ascending order
   b. Places all elements in the XML document in descending order
   c. Places all return values in ascending order by default
   d. Places all return values in descending order by default

5. The where clause
    a. Locates the XML document
    b. Locates the output file
    c. Specifies the filter criteria
    d. All of the above
6. All functions used by an XQuery are built-in functions.
    a. True
    b. False
7. The data() function returns the text value of a variable.
    a. True
    b. False
8. A constructor
    a. Converts information contained in an XML document to another data type
    b. Is the first instance of a function
    c. Is the first instance of a variable
    d. None of the above
9. The doc() function retrieves an XML document.
    a. True
    b. False
10. The round-half-to-even() function rounds half the value returned by a function.
    a. True
    b. False

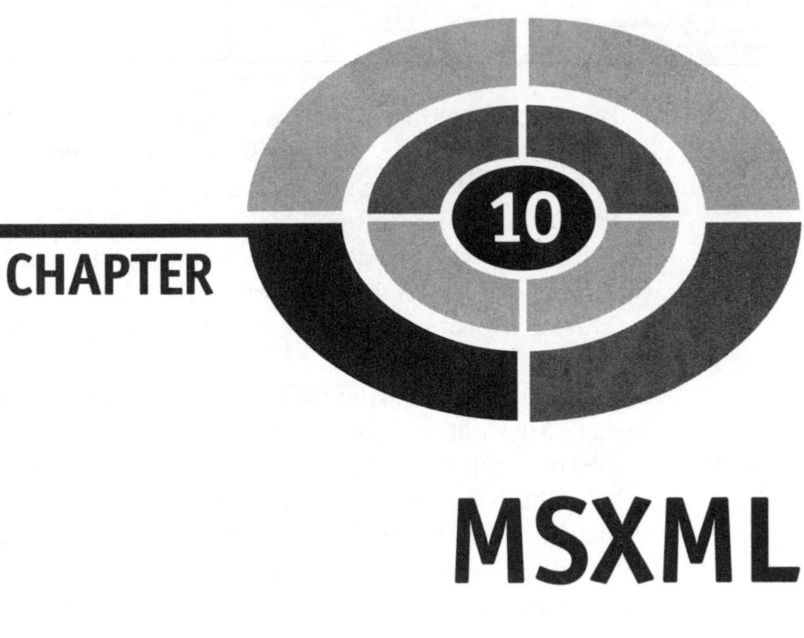

MSXML

You combine the power of XML and programming languages such as JavaScript, Visual Basic, and C++ when you use Microsoft's XML Core Services, simply referred to as MSXML. MSXML is an application program interface that contains features that enable you to interact with XML from within an application written in one of the commonly used programming languages.

This means that you can unleash an XML document from within a program rather than having to use a web browser. You can easily integrate any XML document into your application by calling features of MSXML from within your program.

You'll learn about MSXML in this chapter and how to access an XML document using JavaScript. The same basic principles used for JavaScript can be applied to other programming languages.

What Is MSXML?

XML is a dynamic approach to managing information. As you've learned throughout this book, you can access an XML document using an XML-enabled browser. This is fine if you want to display all or a portion of an XML document. Simply follow the directions we present in this book and you're able to view information contained in the XML document from your browser.

However, accessing an XML document using an application other than a browser can be tricky because code must be written within the application to extract information contained in the XML document.

Fortunately, Microsoft provides the magic wand to take the pain out of writing code to access an XML document from within an application with Microsoft XML Core Services—MSXML for short. MSXML consists of preprogrammed classes and functions that contain code to access and manipulate information in an XML document.

You don't have to write the tedious code to read and parse an XML document because Microsoft has done this for you. All you need to do is to call the appropriate classes or functions within your application to work with an XML document.

MSXML is designed for a variety of programming languages, including C, C++, Visual Basic, VBScript, Jscript, and JavaScript. You can download the MSXML API at http://msdn.microsoft.com/xml/default.aspx, and will need to do so before you can use the examples we illustrate in this chapter.

We use JavaScript as the programming language for this chapter because you don't need to use a compiler to create a JavaScript application. You simply write the code using the same editor that you use to write your web page. JavaScript is executed by calling the JavaScript from a web page using your browser.

We'll show you a few JavaScript basics in this chapter—enough so you can get started using MSXML. However, you may want to read *JavaScript Demystified* by Jim Keogh (McGraw-Hill Osborne Media, 2005) to become proficient using JavaScript.

You'll need to install the MSXML API or download it from the Microsoft web site. We're using version 4.0; however, you should download the latest release.

Getting Down and Dirty with MSXML

Let's jump in. To start learning MSXML, you'll first create an XML document. The XML document is a catalog of CDs that we'll simply call catalog.xml. It contains seven CDs, as you'll see in the code that follows. Enter this XML code into a file and save it to your drive. Be sure to call the file catalog.xml.

```
<?xml version="1.0"?>
<!DOCTYPE catalog SYSTEM "catalog.dtd">
<catalog>
   <cd upc="602498678299">
      <artist>U2</artist>
      <title>How to Dismantle an Atomic Bomb</title>
      <price>13.98</price>
      <label>Interscope Records</label>
      <date>2004-11-23</date>
```

```
    </cd>
    <cd upc="75679244222">
        <artist>Led Zeppelin</artist>
        <title>Physical Graffiti</title>
        <price>22.99</price>
        <label>Atlantic</label>
        <date>1994-08-16</date>
    </cd>
    <cd upc="75678367229">
        <artist>Rush</artist>
        <title>Rush in Rio</title>
        <price>13.98</price>
        <label>Atlantic</label>
        <date>2003-10-21</date>
    </cd>
    <cd upc="74646938720">
        <artist>Billy Joel</artist>
        <title>Songs in the Attic</title>
        <price>10.99</price>
        <label>Sony</label>
        <date>1998-10-20</date>
    </cd>
    <cd upc="75678263927">
        <artist>Led Zeppelin</artist>
        <title>Houses of the Holy</title>
        <price>10.98</price>
        <label>Atlantic</label>
        <date>1994-07-19</date>
    </cd>
    <cd upc="8811160227">
        <artist>Jimi Hendrix</artist>
        <title>Are You Experienced?</title>
        <price>12.99</price>
        <label>Experience Hendrix</label>
        <date>1997-04-22</date>
    </cd>
    <cd upc="74640890529">
        <artist>Bob Dylan</artist>
        <title>The Times They Are A-Changin'</title>
        <price>9.99</price>
        <label>Sony</label>
        <date>1990-10-25</date>
    </cd>
</catalog>
```

You'll notice that the XML document refers to the catalog.dtd. As you'll recall from Chapter 3, a DTD file contains the document type definition that defines the markup tags that can be used in the XML document and specifies the parent-child structure of those tags. The XML parser references the DTD when parsing elements of the XML document.

Create a DTD for this example. You do this by writing the following information into a file and saving the file as catalog.dtd in the directory that contains the catalog .xml file.

```
<!ELEMENT catalog (cd*)>
<!ELEMENT cd (artist, title, price, label, date)>
<!ELEMENT artist (#PCDATA)>
<!ELEMENT title (#PCDATA)>
<!ELEMENT price (#PCDATA)>
<!ELEMENT label (#PCDATA)>
<!ELEMENT date (#PCDATA)>
<!ATTLIST cd
   upc CDATA #REQUIRED>
```

The final step you'll take to prepare to learn MSXML is to create the HTML file that contains the JavaScript used to access the catalog.xml document. The HTML file follows. Some of it is familiar because it's HTML. Other parts, you'll understand if you know JavaScript (don't worry if you don't understand them; we explain JavaScript throughout this chapter). However, the portions of the HTML file that use MSXML are probably confusing, even if you previously worked with JavaScript.

For now, simply create this HTML file and save it to a file called default.html in the directory where you saved catalog.xml and catalog.dtd. We explain each part of the HTML file throughout this chapter.

```
<html>
<head>
<script language="javascript">
var objXML;
function LoadDocument()
{
   var inputfile = document.all("inputfile").value;
   objXML = new ActiveXObject("MSXML2.DOMDocument.4.0");
   objXML.async = false;
   objXML.load(inputfile);
   if (objXML.parseError.errorCode != 0)
   {
      alert("Error loading input file: " + objXML.parseError.reason);
      return;
   }
   document.all("xmldoc").value = objXML.xml;
}
```

```
function InsertFirst()
{
   var objNewNode = LoadNewNode();
   if(objNewNode == null)
   {
       return;
   }
   var root = objXML.documentElement;
   root.insertBefore(objNewNode, root.firstChild);
   document.all("xmlresult").value = objXML.xml;
}
function InsertLast()
{
   var objNewNode = LoadNewNode();
   if(objNewNode == null)
   {
      return;
   }
   var root = objXML.documentElement;
   root.appendChild(objNewNode);
   document.all("xmlresult").value = objXML.xml;
}
function InsertBefore(upc)
{
   var objNewNode = LoadNewNode();
   if(objNewNode == null)
   {
      return;
   }
   var root = objXML.documentElement;
   var objNodes = objXML.selectNodes("/catalog/cd[@upc='" + upc + "']");
   if(objNodes.length == 0)
   {
      alert("Could not find node with upc " + upc);
      return;
   }
   root.insertBefore(objNewNode, objNodes.item(0));
   document.all("xmlresult").value = objXML.xml;
}
function InsertAfter(upc)
{
   var objNewNode = LoadNewNode();
   if(objNewNode == null)
   {
      return;
   }
   var root = objXML.documentElement;
   var childNodes = root.childNodes;
   for(var i=0; i < childNodes.length; i++)
   {
      var node = childNodes.item(i);
      var nodeUPC = node.getAttribute("upc");
      if(nodeUPC == upc)
      {
         root.insertBefore(objNewNode, childNodes.item(i+1));
```

```
            document.all("xmlresult").value = objXML.xml;
            return;
         }
      }
      alert("Could not find node with upc " + upc);
   }
   function LoadNewNode()
   {
      var xmlNewNode = document.all("newnode").value;
      var objNewNode = new ActiveXObject("MSXML2.DOMDocument.4.0");
      objNewNode.async = false;
      objNewNode.loadXML(xmlNewNode);
      if (objNewNode.parseError.errorCode != 0)
      {
         alert("Error loading new node: " + objNewNode.parseError.reason);
         return null;
      }
      else
      {
         return objNewNode.documentElement;
      }
   }
   function CreateAndAppendNode()
   {
      var upc = document.all("createUpc").value;
      var artist = document.all("createArtist").value;
      var title = document.all("createTitle").value;
      var price = document.all("createPrice").value;
      var label = document.all("createLabel").value;
      var date = document.all("createDate").value;
      var elementCd = objXML.createElement("cd");
      elementCd.setAttribute("upc", upc);
      var elementArtist = objXML.createElement("artist");
      var textArtist = objXML.createTextNode(artist);
      elementArtist.appendChild(textArtist);
      elementCd.appendChild(elementArtist);
      var elementTitle = objXML.createElement("title");
      var textTitle = objXML.createTextNode(title);
      elementTitle.appendChild(textTitle); elementCd.appendChild(elementTitle);
      var elementPrice = objXML.createElement("price");
      var textPrice = objXML.createTextNode(price);
      elementPrice.appendChild(textPrice);
      elementCd.appendChild(elementPrice);
      var elementLabel = objXML.createElement("label");
      var textLabel = objXML.createTextNode(label);
      elementLabel.appendChild(textLabel);
      elementCd.appendChild(elementLabel);
      var elementDate = objXML.createElement("date");
      var textDate = objXML.createTextNode(date);
      elementDate.appendChild(textDate);
      elementCd.appendChild(elementDate);
      var root = objXML.documentElement;
      root.appendChild(elementCd);
      document.all("xmlresult").value = objXML.xml;
   }
```

```
function SelectArtist(artist)
{
    var objNodes = objXML.selectNodes
       ("/catalog/cd[artist='" + artist + "']");
    if(objNodes.length == 0)
    {
       alert("Could not find artist with name " + artist);
       return;
    }
    var root = objXML.documentElement;
    var cdList = root.selectNodes("/catalog/cd");
    cdList.removeAll();
    for(var i=0; i < objNodes.length; i++)
    {
       root.appendChild(objNodes.item(i));
    }
    document.all("xmlresult").value = objXML.xml;
}
function DisplayTitles()
{
   var result = "";
   var objNodes = objXML.selectNodes("/catalog/cd/title");
   for(var i=0; i < objNodes.length; i++)
   {
      result += objNodes.item(i).text + "\r\n";
   }
   document.all("xmlresult").value = result;
}
function DeleteNodes(upc)
{
   var objNodes = objXML.selectNodes("/catalog/cd[@upc='" + upc + "']");
   if(objNodes.length == 0)
   {
      alert("Could not find node with upc " + upc);
      return;
   }
   for(var i=0; i < objNodes.length; i++)
   {
      objXML.documentElement.removeChild(objNodes.item(i));
   }
   document.all("xmlresult").value = objXML.xml;
}
function ValidateDocument()
{
   var err = objXML.validate();
   if (err.errorCode == 0)
   {
      alert("Document is valid.");
   }
   else
   {
      alert("Error validating document:" + err.reason);
   }
}
function TransformDocument(stylesheet)
```

```
{
   var xslProcessor;
   var xslTemplate = new ActiveXObject("Msxml2.XSLTemplate.4.0");
   var xslDocument = new ActiveXObject(
       "Msxml2.FreeThreadedDOMDocument.4.0");
   xslDocument.async = false;
   xslDocument.loadXML(stylesheet);
   if (xslDocument.parseError.errorCode != 0)
   {
      var myErr = xmlDoc.parseError;
      alert("You have error " + myErr.reason);
      return;
   }
   xslTemplate.stylesheet = xslDocument;
   xslProcessor = xslTemplate.createProcessor();
   xslProcessor.input = objXML;
   xslProcessor.transform();
   window.frames.htmlresult.document.open();
   window.frames.htmlresult.document.clear();
   window.frames.htmlresult.document.write(xslProcessor.output);
   window.frames.htmlresult.close();
}
</script>
</head>
<body onload="LoadDocument();">
<table cellpadding="5">
<tr>
<td nowrap>File name: <input type="text"
      id="inputfile" value="catalog.xml"></td>
<td><input type="button" onclick="LoadDocument();"
     value="Load Document"></td>
</tr>
<tr valign="top">
<td>XML Document:</td>
<td><textarea id="xmldoc" rows="20" cols="80" readonly>
    </textarea></td>
</tr>
<tr valign="top">
<td nowrap>
<a href="#" onclick="InsertFirst(); return false;">
    Insert First:</a><br>
<a href="#" onclick="InsertLast(); return false;">
    Insert Last:</a><br>
<a href="#" onclick="InsertBefore(
    document.all('upcBefore').value);
     return false;">Insert Before UPC:</a>
   <input type="text" id="upcBefore"
         value="75678367229" size="15"><br>
         <a href="#" onclick=
         "InsertAfter(document.all('upcAfter').value);
         return false;">Insert After UPC:</a>
   <input type="text" id="upcAfter"
         value="75678367229" size="15"><br>
</td>
<td><textarea id="newnode" rows="10" cols="80">
```

```
<cd upc="75596280822">
   <artist>Phish</artist>
   <title>Live Phish, Vol. 15</title>
   <price>26.99</price>
   <label>ELEKTRA/WEA</label>
   <date>2002-10-29</date>
</cd>
</textarea>
</td>
</tr>
<tr valign="top">
<td nowrap><a href="#" onclick="CreateAndAppendNode();
    return false">Create/Append Node</a></td>
<td nowrap>
upc: <input type="text" id="createUpc"
    value="75596280822" size="15"><br>
artist: <input type="text" id="createArtist"
    value="Phish" size="15"><br>
title: <input type="text" id="createTitle"
    value="Live Phish, Vol. 15" size="15"><br>
price: <input type="text" id="createPrice"
    value="26.99" size="15"><br>
label: <input type="text" id="createLabel"
    value="ELEKTRA/WEA" size="15"><br>
date: <input type="text" id="createDate"
    value="2002-10-29" size="15">
</td>
</tr>
<tr valign="top">
<td colspan="2" nowrap>
<a href="#" onclick="
    SelectArtist(document.all('artist').value);
    return false;">Select Artist:</a>
      <input type="text" id="artist" value="U2" size="15"><br>
<a href="#" onclick="DisplayTitles();
    return false;">Display Titles</a><br>
<a href="#" onclick=
    "DeleteNodes(document.all('upcDelete').value);
    return false;">Delete Nodes w/UPC:</a>
      <input type="text" id="upcDelete"
    value="75678367229" size="15"><br>
<a href="#" onclick="ValidateDocument();
    return false;">Validate Document</a>
</td>
</tr>
<tr valign="top">
<td nowrap><a href="#"
     onclick="TransformDocument(document.all('stylesheet').value);
    return false;">Transform Document:</a></td>
<td>
<textarea id="stylesheet" rows="20" cols="80">
<?xml version="1.0"?>
<xsl:stylesheet version="1.0"
    xmlns:xsl="http://www.w3.org/1999/XSL/Transform">
<xsl:template match="/">
```

```
<html>
   <body>
      <h2>CD Listing</h2>
      <table border="1">
         <tr>
            <th align="center">UPC</th>
            <th align="center">Artist</th>
            <th align="center">Title</th>
        </tr>
        <xsl:for-each select="catalog/cd">
        <tr>
           <td>
              <xsl:value-of select="@upc"/>
           </td>
           <td>
              <xsl:value-of select="artist"/>
           </td>
           <td>
              <xsl:value-of select="title"/>
           </td>
         </tr>
         </xsl:for-each>
      </table>
   </body>
</html>
</xsl:template>
</xsl:stylesheet>
</textarea>
</td>
</tr>
<tr valign="top">
<td>XML Result:</td>
<td><textarea id="xmlresult" rows="20" cols="80"></textarea></td>
</tr>
<tr valign="top">
<td>HTML Result:</td>
<td><iframe id="htmlresult"
   src="about:blank" width="100%" height="300"></td>
</tr>
</table>
</body>
</html>
```

Loading a Document

Let's begin by loading the XML document from the file system into the browser. You accomplish this by entering the name of the XML document into the File name: input field on the HTML form and then selecting the button to refresh the document. These two lines of code within the HTML document create these elements:

```
<td nowrap>File name: <input type="text"
      id="inputfile" value="catalog.xml"></td>
<td><input type="button" onclick="LoadDocument();
      " value="Load Document"></td>
```

The first line creates the input field, and the second line creates the button.

Look at the opening <body> tag on the HTML document and you'll see that you tell the browser to call the LoadDocument() JavaScript function each time that the HTML page is loaded into the browser. This causes the browser to load the default file and display it in the text area of the web page.

```
<body onload="LoadDocument();">
```

Notice that the onclick attribute of the input button also calls the LoadDocument() function when the button is selected. This time the LoadDocument() function loads the file that's named in the File name: input box, which is then displayed in the text area of the web page replacing the current file. You may want to use this button periodically to refresh the XML document to its original state.

The LoadDocument() Function

A function is a piece of code that contains one or more lines of code that execute only if the function is called by another part of the application. Each function has a unique name that's used to call it. A function is defined before it's called. You'll notice that the LoadDocument() function is defined at the beginning of the HTML file.

LoadDocument() is a JavaScript function that loads a document. Here's what it looks like:

```
var objXML;
function LoadDocument()
{
   var inputfile = document.all("inputfile").value;
   objXML = new ActiveXObject("MSXML2.DOMDocument.4.0");
   objXML.async = false;
   objXML.load(inputfile);
   if (objXML.parseError.errorCode != 0)
   {
      alert("Error loading input file: " + objXML.parseError.reason);
      return;
   }
   document.all("xmldoc").value = objXML.xml;
}
```

There are two components shown in this example. The first is objXML. This is a *variable*. Think of a variable as a placeholder for a real value. The objXML is a global variable defined outside the function definition, which means that it can be accessed from anywhere in the application. In contrast, inputfile is a local variable to the LoadDocument() function and is only accessible from within the LoadDocument() function definition.

The second component in this example is the function definition. The function is called LoadDocument(). Code between the French braces ({ }) executes each time another part of the application calls the LoadDocument() function.

The first line in the LoadDocument() function definition accesses the value of the inputfile input box on the HTML form. This is the input box containing the name of the document to load. The *value* is the name of the document. This file name is assigned to a variable called inputfile.

The second line assigns the objXML variable to an instance of the MSXML DOM Object. This function begins by finding out which file to load, which is then stored to the inputfile. Next, you create an ActiveX object for the DOM parser (see Chapter 7). The version number is supplied because MSXML is designed to coexist with previous versions rather than replace a previous version with the latest version.

TIP *Visual Basic, VBScript, C, and C++ access objects using either the ActiveX or COM interface.*

The third line determines if the file is being accessed synchronously or asynchronously. The DOMDocument object contains properties and functions (sometimes called methods). One of those properties is called *async*; it controls how the document is going to behave with your application. By setting the async property to false, you're saying that you want to wait until the document is loaded before executing the next line of code. If you set the async property to true, then the next line of code executes while the document is still loading.

The fourth line calls the load() method, which is defined in the MSXML API. Notice that the inputfile variable is placed between the parentheses of the load() function. This is referred to as passing a variable. In other words, you're passing the name of the file that you want the load() function to load. The file name is the URL to the document. You can replace this with any valid URL to load the document.

The fifth line checks for errors to make sure the document loaded properly. This is done by using an if statement. An *if statement* evaluates a condition. If the condition is true, then code within the French braces is executed; otherwise the code is skipped. In this example, the if statement determines if an error occurred opening the file. If so, then an error message is displayed and the function is terminated. If not, then the application skips to the line following the closed French brace (}). The DOMDocument object has a property called parseError that contains

details of any errors that might have occurred. This is an instance of the IXMLDOMParseError object. It checks if the errorCode is not zero, which means an error occurred. If so, then the error message is displayed on the screen.

The sixth line displays the XML document in the text area of the HTML page. Look carefully and you'll notice that the line references the XML property of the objXML variable. Remember that the objXML variable references the DOMDocument. The XML property of the DOMDocument contains the XML representation of the DOMDocument. Remember, the DOM is a tree type structure. The XML property essentially serializes the DOM back to its familiar markup form.

Adding a New Element

The XML document contains information about CDs. Each CD has a upc attribute and five child elements. Add the following CD to the catalog:

```
<cd upc="75596280822">
   <artist>Phish</artist>
   <title>Live Phish, Vol. 15</title>
   <price>26.99</price>
   <label>ELEKTRA/WEA</label>
   <date>2002-10-29</date>
</cd>
```

You'll need to use four different functions to determine where to place the new CD within the XML document. These functions are

- **InsertFirst()** Put the new entry at the beginning of the list
- **InsertLast()** Put the new entry at the end of the list
- **InsertBefore()** Put the new entry before the CD with the given upc attribute
- **InsertAfter()** Put the new entry after the CD with the given upc attribute

Each function is called by an option on the HTML form. Options appear in the first column of the table. The user of the application decides the position of the new CD within the XML document by selecting the appropriate option.

The first two options place the new CD at the beginning or at the end of the XML document, respectively. The last two options require the user to specify a UPC. The UPC is the identifier for a CD that's already in the XML document. The function then places the new CD either before or after the CD that the user specifies.

The second column contains a text area containing information about the new CD. We've provided a default value when the page loads, but you can change this in the browser. Each function references the text area value when inserting the new CD into the XML document.

```
<tr valign="top">
<td nowrap>
<a href="#" onclick="InsertFirst();
   return false;">Insert First:</a><br>
<a href="#" onclick="InsertLast();
   return false;">Insert Last:</a><br>
<a href="#" onclick="InsertBefore(document.all('upcBefore').value);
   return false;">Insert Before UPC:</a>
   <input type="text" id="upcBefore"
      value="75678367229" size="15"><br>
<a href="#" onclick="InsertAfter(document.all('upcAfter').value);
   return false;">Insert After UPC:</a>
   <input type="text" id="upcAfter"
      value="75678367229" size="15"><br>
</td>
<td><textarea id="newnode" rows="10" cols="80">
<cd upc="75596280822">
   <artist>Phish</artist>
   <title>Live Phish, Vol. 15</title>
   <price>26.99</price>
   <label>ELEKTRA/WEA</label>
   <date>2002-10-29</date>
</cd>
</textarea>
</td>
</tr>
```

The LoadNewNode() Function

The InsertFirst(), InsertLast(), InsertBefore(), and InsertAfter() functions must retrieve information about the new CD from the text area. This is done by calling the LoadNewNode() method. The LoadNewNode() method loads information about the new CD from the text area into the DOM parser and then returns a reference to the root node of the information about the new CD to one of the four functions that called it. Here's the LoadNewNode() method:

```
function LoadNewNode()
{
   var xmlNewNode = document.all("newnode").value;
   var objNewNode = new ActiveXObject("MSXML2.DOMDocument.4.0");
   objNewNode.async = false;
   objNewNode.loadXML(xmlNewNode);
   if (objNewNode.parseError.errorCode != 0)
   {
      alert("Error loading new node: " + objNewNode.parseError.reason);
      return null;
   }
```

```
        else
        {
            return objNewNode.documentElement;
        }
}
```

The first line retrieves text from the text area on the HTML form.

The second line creates a new DOMDocument object that contains information about the new CD.

The third line sets the value for the async property to false so that the entire document loads before returning control to the calling point.

The fourth line calls the loadXML() method of the DOMDocument object. The loadXML() method works similarly to the load() method called within the LoadDocument() function except the loadXML() method is used when the argument is a string. In this case, you're passing the actual XML document as an argument instead of passing a URL that points to the document.

The fifth line checks if an error occurred when loading information about the new CD. If there is an error, then an error message is displayed. If there isn't an error, then the value of the documentElement of the DOMDocument is returned to the statement that called the LoadNewNode() method. The documentElement is the root element of the document, which is a reference to the <cd> element and all its child elements.

The InsertFirst() Method

The InsertFirst() method is called when the user decides to place information about the new CD at the beginning of the XML document. Here's the InsertFirst() method:

```
function InsertFirst()
{
   var objNewNode = LoadNewNode();
   if(objNewNode == null)
   {
      return;
   }
   var root = objXML.documentElement;
   root.insertBefore(objNewNode, root.firstChild);
   document.all("xmlresult").value = objXML.xml;
}
```

The first line calls the LoadNewNode() method, which returns a reference to the root node of the information about the new CD. The reference is assigned to the objNewNode variable.

The second line determines if the value of the objNewNode is null. It's null if the LoadNewNode() method doesn't return a reference to the root node. If this happens, then the InsertFirst() method returns without inserting information about the new CD at the beginning of the XML document.

The third line is executed if the LoadNewNode() method returns a root node. The root node is a reference to an IXMLDOMElement object. This line assigns the value of the IXMLDOMElement object's documentElement property of the new CD information to a variable called root.

The fourth line calls the insertBefore() method of the IXMLDOMElement object. The insertBefore() method has two arguments. The first argument is a reference to the node that's being inserted into the document. This reference is returned by the LoadNewNode() method. The second argument is the node that will come after the new CD in the XML document.

The first CD in the XML document is 602498678299 (see the "Getting Down and Dirty with MSXML" section earlier in this chapter). The new CD will be inserted before CD 602498678299, making the new CD appear first in the XML document and CD 602498678299 second.

The second argument to the insertBefore() method is reference to CD 602498678299. CD 602498678299 is first in the XML document and, therefore, it can be identified by using the firstChild property of the IXMLDOMElement object.

The fifth line displays the code output of the XML representation of the DOMDocument into the text area of the HTML form. The output looks something like this:

```
<?xml version="1.0"?>
<!DOCTYPE catalog SYSTEM "catalog.dtd">
<catalog>
   <cd upc="75596280822">
      <artist>Phish</artist>
         <title>Live Phish, Vol. 15</title>
         <price>26.99</price>
         <label>ELEKTRA/WEA</label>
         <date>2002-10-29</date>
   </cd>
   <cd upc="602498678299">
      <artist>U2</artist>
      <title>How to Dismantle an Atomic Bomb</title>
      <price>13.98</price>
      <label>Interscope Records</label>
      <date>2004-11-23</date>
   </cd>
```

```
    <cd upc="75679244222">
        <artist>Led Zeppelin</artist>
        <title>Physical Graffiti</title>
        <price>22.99</price>
        <label>Atlantic</label>
        <date>1994-08-16</date>
    </cd>
    <cd upc="75678367229">
        <artist>Rush</artist>
        <title>Rush in Rio</title>
        <price>13.98</price>
        <label>Atlantic</label>
        <date>2003-10-21</date>
    </cd>
    <cd upc="74646938720">
        <artist>Billy Joel</artist>
        <title>Songs in the Attic</title>
        <price>10.99</price>
        <label>Sony</label>
        <date>1998-10-20</date>
    </cd>
    <cd upc="75678263927">
        <artist>Led Zeppelin</artist>
        <title>Houses of the Holy</title>
        <price>10.98</price>
        <label>Atlantic</label>
        <date>1994-07-19</date>
    </cd>
    <cd upc="8811160227">
        <artist>Jimi Hendrix</artist>
        <title>Are You Experienced?</title>
        <price>12.99</price>
        <label>Experience Hendrix</label>
        <date>1997-04-22</date>
    </cd>
    <cd upc="74640890529">
        <artist>Bob Dylan</artist>
        <title>The Times They Are A-Changin'</title>
        <price>9.99</price>
        <label>Sony</label>
        <date>1990-10-25</date>
    </cd>
</catalog>
```

The InsertLast() Method

The InsertLast() method is called when the user wants to place information about the new CD at the bottom of the XML document. Here's the InsertLast() method:

```
function InsertLast()
{
   var objNewNode = LoadNewNode();
   if(objNewNode == null)
   {
      return;
   }
   var root = objXML.documentElement;
   root.appendChild(objNewNode);
   document.all("xmlresult").value = objXML.xml;
}
```

You'll notice that the InsertLast() method is nearly the same as the InsertFirst() method, except the appendChild() method is called instead of calling the insertBefore() method. The appendChild() method places information about the new CD at the end of the XML document.

The appendChild() method requires one argument, which is reference to information about the new CD. This reference is returned by the LoadNewNode() method.

Here's the XML document after calling the InsertLast() method. You'll notice that the first and last items in the XML document are the same CD because in our example we selected the InsertFirst option and then the InsertLast option. Each placed the same CD into different areas of the XML document. We've shown it this way to demonstrate that you can continue altering the document to get it into its desired final state. For the remaining examples, refresh the document using the LoadDocument() function so it only shows the current change.

```
<?xml version="1.0"?>
<!DOCTYPE catalog SYSTEM "catalog.dtd">
<catalog>
   <cd upc="75596280822">
      <artist>Phish</artist>
      <title>Live Phish, Vol. 15</title>
      <price>26.99</price>
      <label>ELEKTRA/WEA</label>
      <date>2002-10-29</date>
   </cd>
   <cd upc="602498678299">
      <artist>U2</artist>
```

```
      <title>How to Dismantle an Atomic Bomb</title>
      <price>13.98</price>
      <label>Interscope Records</label>
      <date>2004-11-23</date>
   </cd>
   <cd upc="75679244222">
      <artist>Led Zeppelin</artist>
      <title>Physical Graffiti</title>
      <price>22.99</price>
      <label>Atlantic</label>
      <date>1994-08-16</date>
   </cd>
   <cd upc="75678367229">
      <artist>Rush</artist>
      <title>Rush in Rio</title>
      <price>13.98</price>
      <label>Atlantic</label>
      <date>2003-10-21</date>
   </cd>
   <cd upc="74646938720">
      <artist>Billy Joel</artist>
      <title>Songs in the Attic</title>
      <price>10.99</price>
      <label>Sony</label>
      <date>1998-10-20</date>
   </cd>
   <cd upc="75678263927">
      <artist>Led Zeppelin</artist>
      <title>Houses of the Holy</title>
      <price>10.98</price>
      <label>Atlantic</label>
      <date>1994-07-19</date>
   </cd>
   <cd upc="8811160227">
      <artist>Jimi Hendrix</artist>
      <title>Are You Experienced?</title>
      <price>12.99</price>
      <label>Experience Hendrix</label>
      <date>1997-04-22</date>
   </cd>
   <cd upc="74640890529">
      <artist>Bob Dylan</artist>
      <title>The Times They Are A-Changin'</title>
      <price>9.99</price>
```

```
      <label>Sony</label>
      <date>1990-10-25</date>
   </cd>
   <cd upc="75596280822">
      <artist>Phish</artist>
      <title>Live Phish, Vol. 15</title>
      <price>26.99</price>
      <label>ELEKTRA/WEA</label>
      <date>2002-10-29</date>
   </cd>
</catalog>
```

The InsertBefore() Function

The InsertBefore() function is called when the user specifies the position of the new CD in the XML document. The user does this by entering the UPC code of the CD that will come after the new CD in the XML document. Here's the InsertBefore() function:

```
function InsertBefore(upc)
{
   var objNewNode = LoadNewNode();
   if(objNewNode == null)
   {
      return;
   }
   var root = objXML.documentElement;
   var objNodes = objXML.selectNodes(
       "/catalog/cd[@upc='" + upc + "']");
   if(objNodes.length == 0)
   {
       alert("Could not find node with upc " + upc);
       return;
   }
   root.insertBefore(objNewNode, objNodes.item(0));
   document.all("xmlresult").value = objXML.xml;
}
```

The UPC of the CD that will come after the new CD in the XML document is passed as an argument to the InsertBefore() function by the statement that calls the InsertBefore() function (see the "Getting Down and Dirty with MSXML" section in this chapter).

The first four lines of the InsertBefore() function are the same as those for the InsertFirst() and InsertLast() functions.

Line five calls the selectNodes() method of the DOMDocument object. This method requires one argument containing an XPath expression (see Chapter 5) to identify the node that will come after the new CD in the XML document.

This expression says, Look in the /catalog element for a cd element whose upc attribute is equal to the UPC passed to the selectNodes() method. There can be more than one match. Therefore, the selectNodes() method returns a collection that contains references of matching nodes.

Line six evaluates the value of the length property of the node list returned by the selectNodes() method. If the length is zero, then the CD entered by the user can't be located in the XML document and an alert message is displayed; then the function returns to the statement that called it.

Line seven executes if the selectNodes() method returned a node indicating that the CD was found in the XML document. Line seven calls the insertBefore() method, which is also called by the InsertFirst() function and InsertLast() function. The insertBefore() method requires two arguments. The first argument references the new CD and the second argument references the first CD that will come after the new CD in the XML document. The second argument is the first node the collection returned by the selectNodes() method.

Line eight is the same as it was in the previous functions.

Here's the XML document after the InsertBefore() function executes:

```
<?xml version="1.0"?>
<!DOCTYPE catalog SYSTEM "catalog.dtd">
<catalog>
   <cd upc="602498678299">
      <artist>U2</artist>
      <title>How to Dismantle an Atomic Bomb</title>
      <price>13.98</price>
      <label>Interscope Records</label>
      <date>2004-11-23</date>
   </cd>
   <cd upc="75679244222">
      <artist>Led Zeppelin</artist>
      <title>Physical Graffiti</title>
      <price>22.99</price>
      <label>Atlantic</label>
      <date>1994-08-16</date>
   </cd>
```

```
    <cd upc="75596280822">
        <artist>Phish</artist>
        <title>Live Phish, Vol. 15</title>
        <price>26.99</price>
        <label>ELEKTRA/WEA</label>
        <date>2002-10-29</date>
    </cd>
    <cd upc="75678367229">
        <artist>Rush</artist>
        <title>Rush in Rio</title>
        <price>13.98</price>
        <label>Atlantic</label>
        <date>2003-10-21</date>
    </cd>
    <cd upc="74646938720">
        <artist>Billy Joel</artist>
        <title>Songs in the Attic</title>
        <price>10.99</price>
        <label>Sony</label>
        <date>1998-10-20</date>
    </cd>
    <cd upc="75678263927">
        <artist>Led Zeppelin</artist>
        <title>Houses of the Holy</title>
        <price>10.98</price>
        <label>Atlantic</label>
        <date>1994-07-19</date>
    </cd>
    <cd upc="8811160227">
        <artist>Jimi Hendrix</artist>
        <title>Are You Experienced?</title>
        <price>12.99</price>
        <label>Experience Hendrix</label>
        <date>1997-04-22</date>
    </cd>
    <cd upc="74640890529">
        <artist>Bob Dylan</artist>
        <title>The Times They Are A-Changin'</title>
        <price>9.99</price>
        <label>Sony</label>
        <date>1990-10-25</date>
    </cd>
</catalog>
```

The InsertAfter() Function

The InsertAfter() function is called when the user specifies a CD in the XML document that comes before the new CD. Here's the InsertAfter() function:

```
function InsertAfter(upc)
{
   var objNewNode = LoadNewNode();
   if(objNewNode == null)
   {
      return;
   }
   var root = objXML.documentElement;
   var childNodes = root.childNodes;
   for(var i=0; i < childNodes.length; i++)
   {
      var node = childNodes.item(i);
      var nodeUPC = node.getAttribute("upc");
      if(nodeUPC == upc)
     {
        root.insertBefore(objNewNode, childNodes.item(i+1));
        document.all("xmlresult").value = objXML.xml;
        return;
     }
   }
      alert("Could not find node with upc " + upc);
}
```

The first three lines are the same as they are in previous functions.

The fourth line assigns the childNodes property of the IXMLDOMElement object to the childNodes variable. The childNodes property contains all the child nodes of the <catalog> element in the document.

The fifth line executes a for loop that steps through each child node looking for the child node whose upc attribute matches the UPC code that the user entered. The item() method is called to retrieve the node from the list. Next, the getAttribute() method is called and passed the name of the attribute whose value you want returned. And then an if statement is used to compare the value of the upc attribute of the current child node to the UPC that the user entered.

If they match, then the insertBefore() method is called to insert the new CD into the XML document. The insertBefore() method requires two arguments. The first argument references information about the new CD and the second argument references the existing node in the XML document. The second argument jumps one node ahead by using i+1. In this way, it's going to the next node and inserting before that. The API does not have an insertAfter() method so this is another way to accomplish the same thing. Suppose you were inserting after the last node in the list. i+1 would not reference a valid node because it's beyond the boundary of the list. The second argument would evaluate to null. When the method sees null as the second argument, it puts the new node last in the list. It's equivalent to calling appendNode(). The XML document is then displayed before the function returns to the statement that called the InsertAfter() function.

If they don't match, then the function returns without changing the XML document.

Here's the XML document after the new CD is inserted:

```
<?xml version="1.0"?>
<!DOCTYPE catalog SYSTEM "catalog.dtd">
<catalog>
   <cd upc="602498678299">
      <artist>U2</artist>
      <title>How to Dismantle an Atomic Bomb</title>
      <price>13.98</price>
      <label>Interscope Records</label>
      <date>2004-11-23</date>
   </cd>
   <cd upc="75679244222">
      <artist>Led Zeppelin</artist>
      <title>Physical Graffiti</title>
      <price>22.99</price>
      <label>Atlantic</label>
      <date>1994-08-16</date>
   </cd>
   <cd upc="75678367229">
      <artist>Rush</artist>
      <title>Rush in Rio</title>
      <price>13.98</price>
      <label>Atlantic</label>
      <date>2003-10-21</date>
   </cd>
   <cd upc="75596280822">
      <artist>Phish</artist>
      <title>Live Phish, Vol. 15</title>
      <price>26.99</price>
      <label>ELEKTRA/WEA</label>
      <date>2002-10-29</date>
   </cd>
   <cd upc="74646938720">
      <artist>Billy Joel</artist>
```

```
      <title>Songs in the Attic</title>
      <price>10.99</price>
      <label>Sony</label>
      <date>1998-10-20</date>
   </cd>
   <cd upc="75678263927">
      <artist>Led Zeppelin</artist>
      <title>Houses of the Holy</title>
      <price>10.98</price>
      <label>Atlantic</label>
      <date>1994-07-19</date>
   </cd>
   <cd upc="8811160227">
      <artist>Jimi Hendrix</artist>
      <title>Are You Experienced?</title>
      <price>12.99</price>
      <label>Experience Hendrix</label>
      <date>1997-04-22</date>
   </cd>
   <cd upc="74640890529">
      <artist>Bob Dylan</artist>
      <title>The Times They Are A-Changin'</title>
      <price>9.99</price>
      <label>Sony</label>
      <date>1990-10-25</date>
   </cd>
</catalog>
```

Create a New Element Programmatically

Now we'll show you how to create a new <cd> element and its child elements and insert them into an XML document using a program. First you'll create an HTML page that contains the input fields where you can enter values for the new CD:

```
<tr valign="top">
   <td nowrap><a href="#" onclick="CreateAndAppendNode();
        return false">Create/Append Node</a></td>
   <td nowrap>
      upc: <input type="text" id="createUpc"
          value="75596280822" size="15"><br>
      artist: <input type="text" id="createArtist"
          value="Phish" size="15"><br>
      title: <input type="text" id="createTitle"
```

```
        value="Live Phish, Vol. 15" size="15"><br>
    price: <input type="text" id="createPrice"
        value="26.99" size="15"><br>
    label: <input type="text" id="createLabel"
        value="ELEKTRA/WEA" size="15"><br>
    date: <input type="text" id="createDate"
        value="2002-10-29" size="15">
   </td>
</tr>
```

You're required to enter six values. These are the upc attribute and values for each of the five child elements. Click the hyperlink once you're finished and the CreateAndAppendNode() function executes. Here's the CreateAndAppendNode() function:

```
function CreateAndAppendNode()
{
   var upc = document.all("createUpc").value;
   var artist = document.all("createArtist").value;
   var title = document.all("createTitle").value;
   var price = document.all("createPrice").value;
   var label = document.all("createLabel").value;
   var date = document.all("createDate").value;

   var elementCd = objXML.createElement("cd");
   elementCd.setAttribute("upc", upc);

   var elementArtist = objXML.createElement("artist");
   var textArtist = objXML.createTextNode(artist);
   elementArtist.appendChild(textArtist);
   elementCd.appendChild(elementArtist);

   var elementTitle = objXML.createElement("title");
   var textTitle = objXML.createTextNode(title);
   elementTitle.appendChild(textTitle);
   elementCd.appendChild(elementTitle);

   var elementPrice = objXML.createElement("price");
   var textPrice = objXML.createTextNode(price);
   elementPrice.appendChild(textPrice);
   elementCd.appendChild(elementPrice);

   var elementLabel = objXML.createElement("label");
   var textLabel = objXML.createTextNode(label);
   elementLabel.appendChild(textLabel);
```

```
    elementCd.appendChild(elementLabel);

    var elementDate = objXML.createElement("date");
    var textDate = objXML.createTextNode(date);
    elementDate.appendChild(textDate);
    elementCd.appendChild(elementDate);

    var root = objXML.documentElement;
    root.appendChild(elementCd);

    document.all("xmlresult").value = objXML.xml;
}
```

The first six lines gather values from the HTML table and assign them to variables.

Line seven calls the createElement() method to create a new element. The createElement() method requires one argument, which is the name of the element that you want to create. In this example, you're creating a cd element. The createElement() method returns a reference to the new element.

Line eight calls the setAttribute() method to assign a value to the attribute of the new element. The setAttribute() method requires two arguments. The first argument is the name of the attribute that's being set and the second argument is the value assigned to the new attribute.

Lines 9 through 30 create child elements for the <cd> element. Notice that each child element is actually two nodes—one for the element and the other for the text. Line 31 displays the XML document, as we show here:

```
<?xml version="1.0"?>
<!DOCTYPE catalog SYSTEM "catalog.dtd">
<catalog>
    <cd upc="602498678299">
        <artist>U2</artist>
        <title>How to Dismantle an Atomic Bomb</title>
        <price>13.98</price>
        <label>Interscope Records</label>
        <date>2004-11-23</date>
    </cd>
    <cd upc="75679244222">
        <artist>Led Zeppelin</artist>
        <title>Physical Graffiti</title>
        <price>22.99</price>
        <label>Atlantic</label>
        <date>1994-08-16</date>
    </cd>
```

```
  <cd upc="75678367229">
    <artist>Rush</artist>
    <title>Rush in Rio</title>
    <price>13.98</price>
    <label>Atlantic</label>
    <date>2003-10-21</date>
  </cd>
  <cd upc="74646938720">
    <artist>Billy Joel</artist>
    <title>Songs in the Attic</title>
    <price>10.99</price>
    <label>Sony</label>
    <date>1998-10-20</date>
  </cd>
  <cd upc="75678263927">
    <artist>Led Zeppelin</artist>
    <title>Houses of the Holy</title>
    <price>10.98</price>
    <label>Atlantic</label>
    <date>1994-07-19</date>
  </cd>
  <cd upc="8811160227">
    <artist>Jimi Hendrix</artist>
    <title>Are You Experienced?</title>
    <price>12.99</price>
    <label>Experience Hendrix</label>
    <date>1997-04-22</date>
  </cd>
  <cd upc="74640890529">
    <artist>Bob Dylan</artist>
    <title>The Times They Are A-Changin'</title>
    <price>9.99</price>
    <label>Sony</label>
   <date>1990-10-25</date>
  </cd>
  <cd upc="75596280822">
   <artist>Phish</artist>
   <title>Live Phish, Vol. 15</title>
   <price>26.99</price>
   <label>ELEKTRA/WEA</label>
   <date>2002-10-29</date>
  </cd>
</catalog>
```

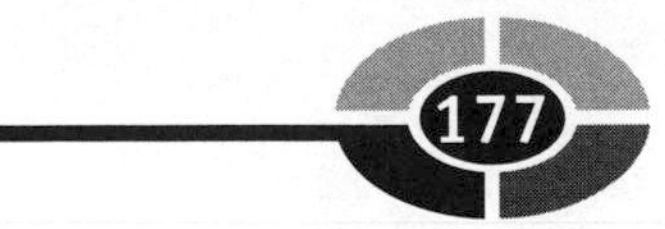

Select, Extract, Delete, and Validate

So far in this chapter, you've learned how to insert one XML document into another. In addition to this, you'll need to select, extract, delete, and validate information contained in an XML document.

We'll explore how to perform these common tasks in this section. First we'll show you how to create an HTML page that enables you to execute each of these tasks. In a real-world application, of course, these tasks would be built into your application.

Here's the HTML page we'll use for these examples:

```
<tr valign="top">
<td colspan="2" nowrap>
<a href="#" onclick="SelectArtist(document.all('artist').value);
   return false;">Select Artist:</a>
   <input type="text" id="artist" value="U2" size="15"><br>
<a href="#" onclick="DisplayTitles();
    return false;">Display Titles</a><br>
<a href="#" onclick="DeleteNodes(
    document.all('upcDelete').value); return
    false;">Delete Nodes w/UPC:</a>
   <input type="text" id="upcDelete"
        value="75678367229" size="15"><br>
<a href="#" onclick="ValidateDocument();
        return false;">Validate Document</a>
</td>
</tr>
```

The SelectArtist() Function—Filtering an XML Document

The SelectArtist() function is used to display information about an artist's CDs by entering the name of the artist and then having the SelectArtist() search and display related information about the artist's CDs. Here's the SelectArtist() function:

```
function SelectArtist(artist)
{
   var objNodes = objXML.selectNodes(
         "/catalog/cd[artist='" + artist + "']")
   if(objNodes.length == 0)
   {
      alert("Could not find artist with name " + artist);
```

```
        return;
    }
    var root = objXML.documentElement;
    var cdList = root.selectNodes("/catalog/cd");
    cdList.removeAll();
    for(var i=0; i < objNodes.length; i++)
    {
        root.appendChild(objNodes.item(i));
    }
    document.all("xmlresult").value = objXML.xml;
}
```

The first line calls the selectNodes() method, which you learned about throughout this chapter. The selectNodes() method requires one argument, which is the XPath expression (see Chapter 5) used to identify the artist. This expression says, Look in the catalog element for a cd element whose artist is equal to the artist entered by the user. The selectNodes() method returns a collection that contains information about all the CDs that are listed for the artist.

The second line examines the length property of the collection, which contains the total number of items returned by the selectNodes() method. If the length is zero, then the artist wasn't found. An alert is displayed on the screen that the function returns without displaying any information.

Line three executes if the length is greater than zero, and assigns reference to the documentElement to the root variable.

Line four calls the selectNodes() method to retrieve information about all the CDs in the document.

Line five calls the removeAll() method, which removes all information about CDs from the XML document. The XML document now looks like this:

```
<?xml version="1.0"?>
<!DOCTYPE catalog SYSTEM "catalog.dtd">
<catalog></catalog>
```

Line six executes a for loop that calls the appendChild node to insert back into the XML document information about CDs from the selected artist. The XML document now looks like this:

```
<?xml version="1.0"?>
<!DOCTYPE catalog SYSTEM "catalog.dtd">
<catalog>
    <cd upc="602498678299">
        <artist>U2</artist>
        <title>How to Dismantle an Atomic Bomb</title>
        <price>13.98</price>
```

```
      <label>Interscope Records</label>
      <date>2004-11-23</date>
   </cd>
</catalog>
```

The DisplayTitles() Function

You use the DisplayTitles() function to copy and display information contained in an XML document, but not alter the original document. Here's the DisplayTitles() function:

```
function DisplayTitles()
{
   var result = "";
   var objNodes = objXML.selectNodes("/catalog/cd/title");
   for(var i=0; i < objNodes.length; i++)
   {
      result += objNodes.item(i).text + "\r\n";
   }
   document.all("xmlresult").value = result;
}
```

You'll notice that the DisplayTitles() function has many components that are found in previous examples shown in this chapter. And although we're retrieving selected titles, you can use the same code to select any element from the XML document by simply replacing the element title with the appropriate element name.

The first line declares a variable. The pair of double quotations indicates an empty string is assigned to the variable to initialize it.

The second line calls the selectNodes() function to retrieve a collection that contains title elements.

The third line steps through the collection and assigns the text value of these elements to the result variable. Notice that it also assigns a \r\n. The \r is a carriage return and the \n is a new line. This simply places each element on its own line when the results are displayed.

The fourth line displays the text of the elements as shown here:

How to Dismantle an Atomic Bomb
Physical Graffiti
Rush in Rio
Songs in the Attic
Houses of the Holy
Are You Experienced?
The Times They Are A-Changin'

The DeleteNodes() Function

The DeleteNodes() function removes a specific node from the XML document. Here's the DeleteNodes() function. You'll notice that it requires one argument, which is the UPC code of the CD that is to be deleted from the XML document.

```
function DeleteNodes(upc)
{
   var objNodes = objXML.selectNodes(
        "/catalog/cd[@upc='" + upc + "']");
   if(objNodes.length == 0)
   {
      alert("Could not find node with upc " + upc);
      return;
   }
   for(var i=0; i < objNodes.length; i++)
   {
      objXML.documentElement.removeChild(objNodes.item(i));
   }
   document.all("xmlresult").value = objXML.xml;
}
```

The first line calls the selectNodes() method and passes it the XPath expression that's used to locate elements whose upc attribute matches the CD UPC the user enters. The selectNodes() method returns a collection containing those elements.

The second line uses an if statement to evaluate if a CD matched the UPC. If not, then the length property is zero, the alert message is displayed, and the function returns without deleting any information from the XML document.

The third line executes only if there are elements to be deleted. It uses a for loop to step through the collection and calls the removeChild() method to remove the element.

The fourth line executes once the final element is deleted. This line displays the results we show here:

```
<?xml version="1.0"?>
<!DOCTYPE catalog SYSTEM "catalog.dtd">
<catalog>
   <cd upc="602498678299">
      <artist>U2</artist>
      <title>How to Dismantle an Atomic Bomb</title>
      <price>13.98</price>
      <label>Interscope Records</label>
      <date>2004-11-23</date>
   </cd>
```

```
  <cd upc="75679244222">
    <artist>Led Zeppelin</artist>
    <title>Physical Graffiti</title>
    <price>22.99</price>
    <label>Atlantic</label>
    <date>1994-08-16</date>
  </cd>
  <cd upc="74646938720">
    <artist>Billy Joel</artist>
    <title>Songs in the Attic</title>
    <price>10.99</price>
    <label>Sony</label>
    <date>1998-10-20</date>
  </cd>
  <cd upc="75678263927">
    <artist>Led Zeppelin</artist>
    <title>Houses of the Holy</title>
    <price>10.98</price>
    <label>Atlantic</label>
   <date>1994-07-19</date>
  </cd>
  <cd upc="8811160227">
    <artist>Jimi Hendrix</artist>
    <title>Are You Experienced?</title>
    <price>12.99</price>
    <label>Experience Hendrix</label>
    <date>1997-04-22</date>
  </cd>
  <cd upc="74640890529">
    <artist>Bob Dylan</artist>
    <title>The Times They Are A-Changin'</title>
    <price>9.99</price>
    <label>Sony</label>
    <date>1990-10-25</date>
  </cd>
</catalog>
```

The ValidateDocument() Function

You use the ValidateDocument() function to validate an XML document against the document's DTD to determine if all elements in the XML document are defined in the DTD. Here's the ValidateDocument() function. Notice that this is one of the simplest functions that you can build. It simply calls the validate() method and then evaluates the return value. If the returned errorCode is zero, then the XML document is valid. If the errorCode is other than zero, then the XML doesn't comply with the DTD.

```
function ValidateDocument()
{
   var err = objXML.validate();
   if (err.errorCode == 0)
   {
      alert("Document is valid.");
   }
   else
   {
      alert("Error validating document:" + err.reason);
   }
}
```

To test this function, return to the InsertFirst() function at the beginning of this chapter. Change the value of the new CD element in the text area of the HTML page to the following. Notice that the price element is deleted. This is required by the DTD.

```
<cd upc="75596280822">
   <artist>Phish</artist>
   <title>Live Phish, Vol. 15</title>
   <label>ELEKTRA/WEA</label>
   <date>2002-10-29</date>
</cd>
```

Click the InsertFirst() hyperlink and the XML document will look like this. Notice that price is missing, making the XML document invalid according to the DTD.

```
<?xml version="1.0"?>
<!DOCTYPE catalog SYSTEM "catalog.dtd">
<catalog>
   <cd upc="75596280822">
      <artist>Phish</artist>
      <title>Live Phish, Vol. 15</title>
      <label>ELEKTRA/WEA</label>
      <date>2002-10-29</date>
   </cd>
   <cd upc="602498678299">
      <artist>U2</artist>
      <title>How to Dismantle an Atomic Bomb</title>
      <price>13.98</price>
      <label>Interscope Records</label>
      <date>2004-11-23</date>
```

```
    </cd>
    <cd upc="75679244222">
       <artist>Led Zeppelin</artist>
       <title>Physical Graffiti</title>
       <price>22.99</price>
       <label>Atlantic</label>
       <date>1994-08-16</date>
    </cd>
    <cd upc="75678367229">
       <artist>Rush</artist>
       <title>Rush in Rio</title>
       <price>13.98</price>
       <label>Atlantic</label>
       <date>2003-10-21</date>
    </cd>
    <cd upc="74646938720">
       <artist>Billy Joel</artist>
       <title>Songs in the Attic</title>
       <price>10.99</price>
       <label>Sony</label>
       <date>1998-10-20</date>
    </cd>
    <cd upc="75678263927">
       <artist>Led Zeppelin</artist>
       <title>Houses of the Holy</title>
       <price>10.98</price>
       <label>Atlantic</label>
       <date>1994-07-19</date>
    </cd>
    <cd upc="8811160227">
       <artist>Jimi Hendrix</artist>
       <title>Are You Experienced?</title>
       <price>12.99</price>
       <label>Experience Hendrix</label>
       <date>1997-04-22</date>
    </cd>
    <cd upc="74640890529">
       <artist>Bob Dylan</artist>
       <title>The Times They Are A-Changin'</title>
       <price>9.99</price>
       <label>Sony</label>
       <date>1990-10-25</date>
    </cd>
</catalog>
```

The DOMDocument object doesn't automatically revalidate the XML document each time it's altered, so no error message is displayed. Now select the Validate Document link on the HTML page. The ValidateDocument() function validates the XML document and displays an alert message indicating that the XML Document is invalid. The alert message is something like:

> Error validating document: Element content is invalid according to the DTD/ Schema. Expecting: price.

This is telling you that the price element was expected.

MSXML and XSLT

MSXML can be used to transform an XML document using XSLT (see Chapter 6). Many times you'll want to transform an XML document to an HTML page so a browser can display it. We'll show you how to do this with MSXML. Here's the table row in the HTML page that contains the XSLT stylesheet:

```
<tr valign="top">
<td nowrap><a href="#"
onclick="TransformDocument(document.all(
    'stylesheet').value); return false;">Transform Document:</a></td>
<td>
<textarea id="stylesheet" rows="20" cols="80">
<?xml version="1.0"?>
<xsl:stylesheet version="1.0" xmlns:xsl=
    "http://www.w3.org/1999/XSL/Transform">
<xsl:template match="/">
<html>
   <body>
   <h2>CD Listing</h2>
   <table border="1">
      <tr>
         <th align="center">UPC</th>
         <th align="center">Artist</th>
         <th align="center">Title</th>
      </tr>
      <xsl:for-each select="catalog/cd">
      <tr>
         <td>
            <xsl:value-of select="@upc"/>
         </td>
         <td>
            <xsl:value-of select="artist"/>
         </td>
         <td>
            <xsl:value-of select="title"/>
         </td>
      </tr>
```

```
        </xsl:for-each>
    </table>
    </body>
</html>
</xsl:template>
</xsl:stylesheet>
</textarea>
</td>
</tr>
```

The second table cell has a text area that contains the stylesheet. We've provided a default stylesheet, but you can change the default in the browser when you're running this example. The first cell takes the stylesheet from the text area and passes it as an argument to the TransformDocument() function. Here's the TransformDocument() function:

```
function TransformDocument(stylesheet)
{
    var xslProcessor;
    var xslTemplate = new ActiveXObject("Msxml2.XSLTemplate.4.0");
    var xslDocument = new ActiveXObject(
         "Msxml2.FreeThreadedDOMDocument.4.0");
    xslDocument.async = false;
    xslDocument.loadXML(stylesheet);
    if (xslDocument.parseError.errorCode != 0)
    {
        var myErr = xmlDoc.parseError;
        alert("You have error " + myErr.reason);
        return;
    }
    xslTemplate.stylesheet = xslDocument;
    xslProcessor = xslTemplate.createProcessor();
    xslProcessor.input = objXML;
    xslProcessor.transform();
    window.frames.htmlresult.document.open();
    window.frames.htmlresult.document.clear();
    window.frames.htmlresult.document.write(xslProcessor.output);
    window.frames.htmlresult.close();
}
```

The first line declares a variable.

The second line creates an XSLTemplate object and assigns it to a variable.

The third line creates a DOMDocument object and assigns it to a variable.

The fourth line sets the async property to false so the next statement doesn't execute until the document is loaded.

The fifth line calls the loadXML() method and passes it the stylesheet.

The sixth line determines if there is an error. If so, then an error message is displayed and the function returns to the statement that called it without transforming the XML document.

The seventh line executes if there isn't an error. This line assigns the xslDocument to the stylesheet property of the xslTemplate.

The eighth line calls the createProcessor() method to create an xslProcessor.

The ninth line assigns the XML document to the input property of the xslProcessor.

The tenth line calls the transform() method to transform the XML document.

Lines 11 through 14 write the transformed XML document to the browser. The results are shown next.

CD Listing

Here is the list of CDs organized by UPC, artist, and title that is produced by using MXSML to transform an XML document using XSLT. This is illustrated in the previous section of this chapter.

UPC	Artist	Title
602498678299	U2	How to Dismantle an Atomic Bomb
75679244222	Led Zeppelin	Physical Graffiti
75678367229	Rush	Rush in Rio
74646938720	Billy Joel	Songs in the Attic
75678263927	Led Zeppelin	Houses of the Holy
8811160227	Jimi Hendrix	Are You Experienced?
74640890529	Bob Dylan	The Times They Are A-Changin'

Summary

In this chapter you learned how to combine the power of XML and the MSXML application program interface that enables you to interact with an XML document from within an application written in one of the popular programming languages.

MSXML enables you to access an XML document by using an application that you create rather than accessing the XML document using a browser. MSXML contains preprogrammed classes and functions that contain code necessary to access and manipulate information in an XML document.

You need to call the appropriate classes and functions from within your application to interact with an XML document without having to write tedious code to read and parse the XML document. MSXML works with C, C++, Visual Basic, VBScript, Jscript, and JavaScript.

Quiz

1. MSXML can only be used with JavaScript.
   a. True
   b. False
2. The async = false means
   a. Statements will continue to execute as the XML document is being loaded.
   b. Statements will not execute until the XML document is being loaded.
   c. The XML document is synchronized to the HTML page.
   d. None of the above.
3. firstChild is a
   a. Property containing a reference to the first child of an element
   b. Method that makes the current node the first child
   c. Method that substitutes the first node for the last node
   d. Method that substitutes the last node for the first node
4. createElement("title") means
   a. Create a new HTML element
   b. Create a new XML element
   c. Create a title for a new HTML element
   d. Create an attribute called title for the current XML element
5. "/catalog/cd[@upc='" + upc + "'] means
   a. Find the text that matches the value of the upc variable in the cd element
   b. Find the upc attribute that matches the value of the upc variable in the cd element
   c. Find the upc element that matches the UPC in the cd element
   d. All of the above
6. An XML document can be validated against a DTD by calling the validate() method.
   a. True
   b. False

7. The appendChild() appends a node to the end of an XML document.
   a. True
   b. False
8. The version is specified in ActiveXObject("MSXML2
   .DOMDocument.4.0") because
   a. Versions are designed to coexist with previous versions.
   b. Only the version specified can be used with the XML document.
   c. It identifies potential conflicts in versions.
   d. None of the above.
9. The loadXML() method is used when the document is passed as a string.
   a. True
   b. False
10. getAttribute("upc") retrieves the value of the upc attribute.
    a. True
    b. False

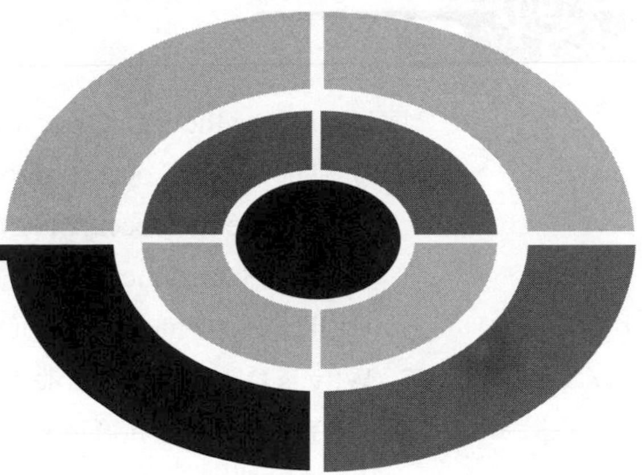

Final Exam

1. SAX can be used to build and alter XML documents.
   a. True
   b. False
2. What does the ? qualifier mean when it's applied to an element in a DTD?
   a. The element occurs zero or one time (optional element).
   b. The element occurs zero to many times.
   c. The element occurs one to many times.
   d. The element occurs exactly one time.
3. What does the + qualifier mean when it's applied to an element in a DTD?
   a. The element occurs zero or one time (optional element).
   b. The element occurs zero to many times.
   c. The element occurs one to many times.
   d. The element occurs exactly one time.

4. What does the * qualifier mean when it's applied to an element in a DTD?
   a. The element occurs zero or one time (optional element).
   b. The element occurs zero to many times.
   c. The element occurs one to many times.
   d. The element occurs exactly one time.
5. Why is DOM not suitable for reading large documents?
   a. The parser is not very efficient.
   b. DOM restricts the size of an XML document.
   c. The entire document is read into memory.
   d. None of the above.
6. Which of the following is a valid XML comment?
   a. <-- comments go here -->
   b. <comment>comments go here</comment>
   c. <!-- comments go here --!>
   d. <!-- comments go here -->
7. What's the difference between CDATA and PCDATA?
   a. CDATA is only used in attributes.
   b. PCDATA is translated for entities.
   c. PCDATA is only used in elements.
   d. None of the above.
8. A CDATA section is translated before being passed to the application.
   a. True
   b. False
9. A CDATA section would be a suitable means of embedding binary data into an XML document.
   a. True
   b. False
10. Which of the following is a valid CDATA section?
    a. <![[CDATA[data goes here]]]>
    b. <!{{CDATA[data goes here }}>
    c. <[[CDATA[data goes here]]>
    d. None of the above

11. Which of the following is a valid processing instruction?
    a. <?xml version="1.0">
    b. <xml version="1.0">
    c. <?xml version="1.0"?>
    d. None of the above
12. Processing instructions that start with "xml" are reserved for current and future standards.
    a. True
    b. False
13. An entity can be used to set default values in an XML document.
    a. True
    b. False
14. What character or word is used for a logical OR operation?
    a. OR
    b. |
    c. &
    d. None of the above
15. What does <!ELEMENT address (mailing|billing|delivery)> tell you about the XML document?
    a. The address element has three child elements for mailing, billing, and delivery.
    b. The mailing, billing, and delivery elements are optional.
    c. The address element has one child element that can be mailing, billing, or delivery.
    d. None of the above.
16. What does <!ELEMENT address (mailing, billing, delivery)> tell you about the XML document?
    a. The address element has three child elements for mailing, billing, and delivery.
    b. The mailing, billing, and delivery elements are optional.
    c. The address element has one child element that can be mailing, billing, or delivery.
    d. None of the above.

17. What does <!ELEMENT address (mailing?, billing?, delivery?)> tell you about the XML document?
    a. The address element has three child elements for mailing, billing, and delivery.
    b. The mailing, billing, and delivery elements are optional.
    c. The address element has one child element that can be mailing, billing, or delivery.
    d. None of the above.
18. What does <!ELEMENT address (mailing, billing, delivery+)> tell you about the XML document?
    a. The address element has three child elements for mailing, billing, and delivery.
    b. The mailing, billing, and delivery elements are optional.
    c. The address element has one child element that can be mailing, billing, or delivery.
    d. None of the above.
19. What does the declaration <!ENTITY % format "(PDF|TXT)"> tell you about the XML document?
    a. The format entity has two child elements.
    b. The allowable values for format are PDF and TXT.
    c. The format entity contains a group of values.
    d. None of the above.
20. A DTD can be used to define a subset of the XML document.
    a. True
    b. False
21. Which of the following is a valid XML schema date field?
    a. 2007-11-17
    b. 11/17/2007
    c. November 17, 2007
    d. 17 November 2007
22. An XML schema is built on top of a DTD.
    a. True
    b. False

23. In the schema tag <xs:element name="format" type="xs:string" fixed="PDF"/>, which of the following is a valid XML fragment?
    a. <string>PDF</string>
    b. <format value="PDF" />
    c. <format>TXT</format>
    d. <format>PDF</format>
24. In the schema tag <xs:element name="format" type="xs:string" default="PDF"/>, which of the following is a valid XML fragment?
    a. <format>HTML</format>
    b. <format>PDF</format>
    c. <format>TXT</format>
    d. All of the above
25. What is the type attribute used for in an XML schema element declaration?
    a. Specifies the type of element
    b. Specifies whether the element is optional or required
    c. Specifies the type of data contained by the element
    d. None of the above
26. In the schema tag <xs:element name="amount" type="xs:decimal"/>, which of the following is a valid XML fragment?
    a. <amount>23.67</amount>
    b. <amount value="23.67" />
    c. <element amount="23.67" />
    d. None of the above
27. In the schema tag <xs:attribute name="size" type="xs:string" default="small"/>, which of the following is a valid XML fragment?
    a. <soda size="medium">
    b. <soda size="large">
    c. <soda size="extra large">
    d. All of the above
28. How do you specify in the schema that an attribute is required?
    a. value="required"
    b. attribute="required"

c. use="required"

d. None of the above

29. What is the restriction tag used for in the schema?

a. Assigning security restrictions to the data

b. Placing restrictions on the values of elements or attributes

c. Restricting where the tag can be placed in the XML document

d. None of the above

30. The schema restriction tag must be followed by one to many enumeration tags.

a. True

b. False

31. What is the equivalent of saying "greater than or equal to 50" in XML schema?

a. <xs:minimum value="50"/>

b. <xs:minExclusive value="50"/>

c. <xs:min value="50"/>

d. <xs:minInclusive value="50"/>

32. What is the equivalent of saying "greater than 50" in XML schema?

a. <xs:minimum value="50"/>

b. <xs:minExclusive value="50"/>

c. <xs:min value="50"/>

d. <xs:minInclusive value="50"/>

33. An enumeration can be used to define multiple discrete values for an attribute.

a. True

b. False

34. Restrictions can only be used with complex types.

a. True

b. False

35. What is the base attribute used for with a restriction?

a. Defining the base schema reference

b. Defining the data type for the restriction

c. Referencing the base restriction

d. None of the above

36. What are three options for dealing with whitespace in an XML schema?

a. retain, replace, remove

b. preserve, replace, delete

c. preserve, replace, collapse

d. retain, replace, collapse

37. Replace tells the parser to replace all whitespace characters with a space.

a. True

b. False

38. Which of the following restricts the length of the value of an element to 40 characters?

a. <xs:length value="40"/>

b. <xs:maxLength value="40"/>

c. <xs:length max="40"/>

d. <xs:string length="40"/>

39. In an XML schema, what attributes are used to define the number of occurrences?

a. minOccurs, maxOccurs

b. min, max

c. minimum, maximum

d. You can't define the number of occurrences in an XML schema.

40. What are the two types of XLinks?

a. Simple and extended

b. Simple and complex

c. Single and multiple

d. None of the above

41. xlink:show="replace" causes what kind of behavior?

a. Replaces one link with another link

b. Replaces the resource with another resource

c. Invalidates the resource

d. None of the above

42. xlink:show="embed" is used to insert a resource at a specified location.
    a. True
    b. False
43. Which xlink:actuate attribute is used to load a resource immediately without any interaction?
    a. onRequest
    b. onLoad
    c. Other
    d. None
44. Which xlink:actuate attribute is used by an event to load a resource after the XML document has loaded?
    a. onRequest
    b. onLoad
    c. Other
    d. None
45. Which xlink:actuate attribute is used when the link is not used to load a resource?
    a. onRequest
    b. onLoad
    c. Other
    d. None
46. What do you use to select all the children elements of the context node?
    a. Child::All
    b. Child*
    c. Child::All()
    d. Child::*
47. The child axis contains all the descendants of the context node.
    a. True
    b. False
48. The attribute axis contains attributes for the context node and all the child nodes.
    a. True
    b. False

49. Which axis contains only the context node?
    a. current
    b. context
    c. self
    d. implied
50. What function returns the last node in a node list?
    a. end()
    b. lastIndex()
    c. last()
    d. None of the above
51. What is returned by the number function when a Boolean true is passed in?
    a. 1
    b. 0
    c. NaN
    d. error
52. What is returned by ceiling(7.15)?
    a. 8
    b. 7.2
    c. 7.1
    d. 7
53. What is returned by floor(7.15)?
    a. 8
    b. 7.2
    c. 7.1
    d. 7
54. What is returned by round(8.5)?
    a. 8
    b. 9
    c. NaN
    d. None of the above

55. What is returned by round(8.2)?
    a. 8
    b. 9
    c. NaN
    d. None of the above
56. What is returned by contains('abc', 'abcdef')?
    a. True
    b. False
57. What is returned by contains('abcdef', 'abc')?
    a. True
    b. False
58. What is returned by substring('Bellevue', 3, 3)?
    a. 'lev'
    b. 'lle'
    c. 'l'
    d. 'vue'
59. What does the position() function return?
    a. The current position within an XML document
    b. The position of a node within a node set
    c. The position of a child node
    d. None of the above
60. How do you match the root of an XML document?
    a. <xsl:template match="root">
    b. <xsl:template match="">
    c. <xsl:template match="*">
    d. <xsl:template match="/">
61. <xsl:choose> is used in conjunction with:
    a. <xsl:if>
    b. <xsl:when> and <xsl:otherwise>
    c. <xsl:else>
    d. None of the above

62. The default sort order when using <xsl:sort> is:
    a. Ascending
    b. Descending
63. What attribute is used with <xsl:sort> to define the type of data being sorted?
    a. datatype
    b. dataType
    c. type
    d. data-type
64. What attribute is used with <xsl:sort> to tell the processor what data is being sorted?
    a. select
    b. data
    c. set
    d. None of the above
65. An XSL template defines a reusable piece of XSL code.
    a. True
    b. False
66. A fatal error stops the SAX parser from continuing.
    a. True
    b. False
67. Which SAX event is called for the text nodes in the document?
    a. startElement()
    b. endElement()
    c. characters()
    d. startDocument()
68. Which SAX event is called for a closing element tag?
    a. startElement()
    b. endElement()
    c. characters()
    d. startDocument()

69. An error stops the SAX parser from continuing.
    a. True
    b. False
70. A warning stops the SAX parser from continuing.
    a. True
    b. False
71. What is the DTD Handler used for in SAX?
    a. Assigning a DTD to an XML document
    b. Providing the DTD definition
    c. Validating the XML document using the DTD
    d. None of the above
72. If an XML tag violates the DTD, the parser will not continue.
    a. True
    b. False
    c. Depends on the violation
73. What is the Entity Resolver used for?
    a. Assisting the parser in locating external resources
    b. Resolving entities in the DTD
    c. Identifying entities in the XML document
    d. Locating entities in the XML document
74. DOM cannot be used to build or alter XML documents.
    a. True
    b. False
75. DOM is best suited for reading large documents.
    a. True
    b. False
76. Given the XML fragment <title>Singing in the Rain</title> how would you extract the name of the title element using DOM?
    a. getAttributes()
    b. getNodeName()
    c. getNodeValue()
    d. getNodeType()

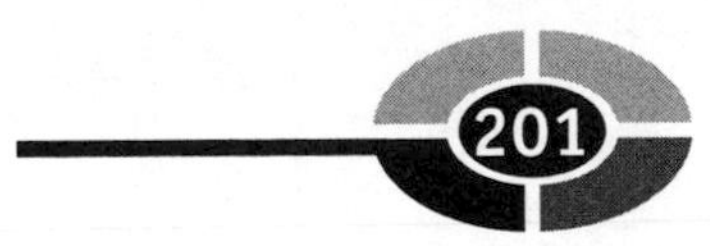

77. Given the XML fragment <title>Singing in the Rain</title> how would you extract the XXXX between the title tags?
    a. getAttributes()
    b. getNodeName()
    c. getNodeValue()
    d. getNodeType()
78. How do you get a list of all the child elements of the current element?
    a. getChildren()
    b. getChildElements()
    c. getChildNodes()
    d. None of the above
79. How do you get the parent of the current node?
    a. parent()
    b. getParentNode()
    c. getParentElement()
    d. None of the above
80. How do you get the grandparent of the current node?
    a. getParents()
    b. getGrandparent()
    c. getAncestors()
    d. None of the above
81. How do you get the node to the right of the current node?
    a. getRight()
    b. getNextSibling()
    c. moveRight()
    d. None of the above
82. How do you get the node to the left of the current node?
    a. getLeft()
    b. getPreviousSibling()
    c. moveLeft()
    d. None of the above

83. Which of the following will link a node to the current node?
    a. appendChild()
    b. linkNode()
    c. addNode()
    d. None of the above
84. The transformer must have a stylesheet in order to perform its transformation.
    a. True
    b. False
85. With RSS, which of the following are valid child elements?
    a. location, link, type
    b. title, link, description
    c. name, description, type
    d. None of the above
86. Which of the following are valid child elements for an RSS image element?
    a. url
    b. title
    c. link
    d. All of the above
87. The <ttl> element specifies the number of milliseconds the document will remain in cache.
    a. True
    b. False
88. What RSS element provides a point of contact if something goes wrong with the feed?
    a. <contact>
    b. <owner>
    c. <webMaster>
    d. None of the above
89. What is contained in the RSS author element?
    a. Name of the author
    b. E-mail address of the author

c. Web site of the feed

d. Phone number of the author

90. What is contained in the RSS item comments element?

a. General comments about the feed

b. URL to a document containing comments

c. Rating for the feed

d. Usage statistics

91. What element is used to include a media file with an item?

a. <attach>

b. <include>

c. <media>

d. <enclosure>

92. The RSS source element is used to identify third-party content.

a. True

b. False

93. XQuery is to XML what SQL is to a relational database.

a. True

b. False

94. The let clause is used to assign variable values.

a. True

b. False

95. What XQuery function do you use to extract text from between the element tags?

a. data()

b. text()

c. extract()

d. value()

96. What is the xs:date() function used for?

a. Returning the current date

b. Returning the creation date of the document

c. Converting a string to a date

d. None of the above

97. Which of the following is a valid XQuery date format?
    a. 2007-03-06
    b. 3/6/2007
    c. None of the above
    d. All of the above
98. The XQuery concat() function is used to concatenate two strings together.
    a. True
    b. False
99. What XQuery function returns the length of a string?
    a. length()
    b. string-length()
    c. strLength()
    d. len()
100. XML is fun.
    a. True
    b. False

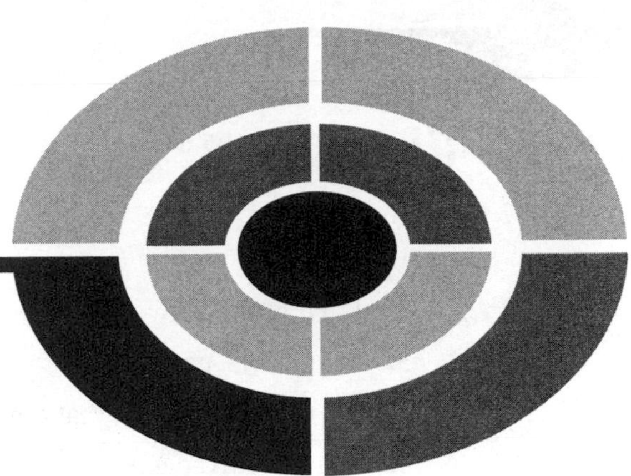

Answers to Quizzes and Final Exam

Chapter 1

1. b. False
2. d. All of the above
3. d. An XML parser
4. b. An XML element that contains parsed character data
5. c. Is an XML parser
6. b. False
7. b. False
8. a. SGML
9. a. True
10. a. True

Chapter 2

1. b. False
2. a. Name/value pair
3. c. The DTD contains zero to many of this element
4. b. Passes the data to the application that uses the XML document without any translation or interpretation
5. c. Identify the DTD for an XML document
6. a. True
7. b. False
8. b. A UNICODE value
9. b. False
10. b. False

Chapter 3

1. b. False
2. c. Parsed character data
3. b. The child element is optional.
4. a. A group
5. c. References a shared DTD
6. a. True
7. b. False
8. d. All of the above
9. b. False
10. a. True

Chapter 4

1. a. True
2. c. Only integers can be used in the corresponding element
3. c. Identify the XML schema specifications used in the XML schema
4. a. Specifies the sequence in which elements must appear in an XML document
5. d. Identify the location of the XML schema
6. a. True
7. a. True
8. a. |
9. a. True.
10. a. True.

Chapter 5

1. a. True
2. a. Associates a local resource with a remote resource
3. d. The link to be loaded into a new window or frame
4. b. At specified times by specifying an attribute to the xlink:actuate element.
5. a. An HTML hyperlink
6. b. False
7. b. False
8. a. The name of the element
9. a. True
10. a. True

Chapter 6

1. b. False
2. a. XSL stylesheet
3. c. For each customer element of the source document that's a child of customers
4. b. Extract text from the source document
5. b. Select the id attribute
6. b. False
7. b. False
8. a. data-type="number"
9. b. False
10. b. False

Chapter 7

1. b. False
2. d. None of the above
3. c. startElement()
4. d. All of the above
5. d. All of the above
6. b. False
7. a. True
8. a. Reads a block of an XML document at a time
9. a. True
10. a. True

Chapter 8

1. a. True
2. c. image
3. c. Tell the aggregator when to find a document that contains comments
4. b. Tell the aggregator days that you don't want the aggregator to update its copy of your RSS document.
5. c. Don't update at 9 p.m.
6. b. False
7. a. True
8. d. All of the above
9. a. True
10. a. True

Chapter 9

1. b. False
2. c. where clause
3. d. Variable
4. c. Places all return values in ascending order by default
5. c. Specifies the filter criteria
6. b. False
7. a. True
8. a. Converts information contained in an XML document to another data type.
9. a. True
10. b. False

Chapter 10

1. b. False
2. b. Statements will not execute until the XML document is being loaded
3. a. Property containing reference to the first child of an element
4. b. Creates a new XML element
5. b. Find the upc attribute that matches the value of the upc variable in the cd element
6. a. True
7. a. True
8. a. Versions are designed to coexist with previous versions.
9. a. True
10. a. True

Final Exam

1. b. False
2. a. The element occurs zero or one time (optional element)
3. c. The element occurs one to many times
4. b. The element occurs zero to many times
5. c. The entire document is read into memory
6. d. <!-- comments go here -->
7. b. PCDATA is translated for entities
8. b. False
9. a. True
10. a. <![[CDATA[data goes here]]]>
11. c. <?xml version="1.0"?>
12. a. True
13. a. True
14. b. |
15. c. The address element has one child element that can be mailing, billing, or delivery.
16. a. The address element has three child elements for mailing, billing, and delivery.
17. b. The mailing, billing, and delivery elements are optional.
18. d. None of the above.
19. b. The allowable values for format are PDF and TXT.
20. a. True
21. a. 2007-11-17
22. a. True
23. d. <format>PDF</format>
24. d. All of the above

25. c. Specifies the type of data contained by the element
26. a. <amount>23.67</amount>
27. d. All of the above
28. c. use="required"
29. b. Placing restrictions on the values of elements or attributes
30. b. False
31. d. <xs:minInclusive value="50"/>
32. b. <xs:minExclusive value="50"/>
33. a. True
34. b. False
35. b. Defining the data type for the restriction
36. c. preserve, replace, collapse
37. a. True
38. b. <xs:maxLength value="40"/>
39. a. minOccurs, maxOccurs
40. b. Simple and complex
41. b. Replaces the resource with another resource
42. a. True
43. b. onLoad
44. a. onRequest
45. d. None
46. d. Child::*
47. a. True
48. b. False
49. c. self
50. c. last()
51. a. 1
52. a. 8
53. d. 7
54. b. 9
55. a. 8

56. b. False
57. a. True
58. b. 'lle'
59. b. The position of a node within a node set
60. d. <xsl:template match="/">
61. b. <xsl:when> and <xsl:otherwise>
62. a. Ascending
63. d. data-type
64. a. select
65. a. True
66. a. True
67. c. characters()
68. b. endElement()
69. b. False
70. b. False
71. c. Validating the XML document using the DTD
72. c. Depends on the violation
73. a. Assisting the parser in locating external resources
74. b. False
75. b. False
76. b. getNodeName()
77. c. getNodeValue()
78. c. getChildNodes()
79. b. getParentNode()
80. d. None of the above
81. b. getNextSibling()
82. b. getPreviousSibling()
83. a. appendChild()
84. b. False
85. b. title, link, description
86. d. All of the above

87. b. False
88. c. <webMaster>
89. b. E-mail address of the author
90. b. URL to a document containing comments
91. d. <enclosure>
92. b. False
93. a. True
94. a. True
95. a. data()
96. c. Converting a string to a date
97. a. 2007-03-06
98. a. True
99. b. string-length()
100. a. True

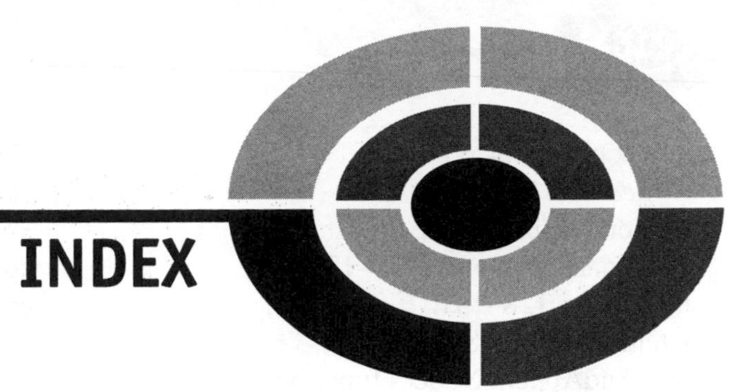

INDEX

R

S

T

U

V

W

X

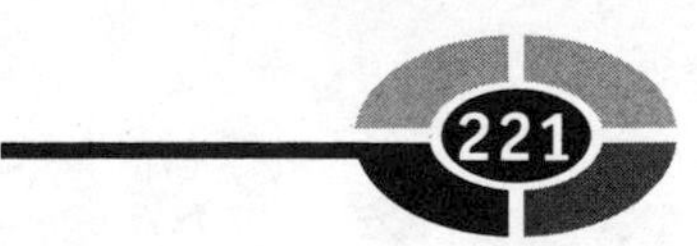